Divination Magic for Beginners

Divination with Runes
A Beginner's Guide to Rune Casting

MONIQUE JOINER SIEDLAK

Oshun
Publications

Divination with Runes © Copyright 2021 by Monique Joiner Siedlak

ISBN: 978-1-950378-71-5

All rights reserved

The content contained within this book may not be reproduced, duplicated or transmitted without direct written permission from the author or the publisher.

Under no circumstances will any blame or legal responsibility be held against the publisher, or author, for any damages, reparation, or monetary loss due to the information contained within this book, either directly or indirectly.

Legal Notice

This book is copyright protected. It is only for personal use. You cannot amend, distribute, sell, use, quote or paraphrase any part, or the content within this book, without the consent of the author or publisher.

Disclaimer Notice

Please note the information contained within this document is for educational and entertainment purposes only. All effort has been executed to present accurate, up to date, reliable, complete information. No warranties of any kind are declared or implied. Readers acknowledge that the author is not engaged in the rendering of legal, financial, medical or professional advice. The content within this book has been derived from various sources. Please consult a licensed professional before attempting any techniques outlined in this book.

By reading this document, the reader agrees that under no circumstances is the author responsible for any losses, direct or indirect, that are incurred as a result of the use of the information contained within this document, including, but not limited to, errors, omissions, or inaccuracies.

Cover Design by MJS

Cover Image by ronin69@depositphotos.com

Published by Oshun Publications

www.oshunpublications.com

Want to learn about Wicca, African Magic, or even Reiki while cleaning your home, exercising, or driving to work? I know it's tough these days to simply find the time to relax and curl up with a good book. This is why I'm delighted to share that I have books available in audiobook format.

Best of all, you can get the audiobook version of this book or any other book by me for free as part of a 30-day Audible trial.

Members get free audiobooks every month and exclusive

discounts. It's an excellent way to explore and determine if audiobook learning works for you.

If you're not satisfied, you can cancel anytime within the trial period. You won't be charged, and you can still keep your book. To choose your free audiobook, visit:

www.mojosiedlak.com/free-audiobooks

Contents

Introduction	ix
1. What Are Runes?	1
2. Runes Lore	13
3. Rune Meanings	23
4. Divination With Runes	35
5. Magic with Runes	41
6. Getting Acquainted With Your Runes	49
7. Casting and Reading	61
8. Storing Your Runes	69
9. Consecrating Your Runes	73
Conclusion	77
References	83
About the Author	85
More Books by Monique	87

Introduction

Throughout the ages, people have sought to communicate through signs, language, and written text. This was more than a form of communication for some; it was a means to create their own destiny by tapping into their own inner powers and harnessing the earth's magic. The runic script and runes were powerful tools, ones which were not only shrouded in mystery but also magic and power. They told stories of Viking Age battles, of conquering lands, and of seeing the future. Runes are some of the earliest forms of divination. The very sight of runic writings on weapons could put fear into an opponent who believed the weapon's yielder was possessed by the power of the gods. This book will delve into the science and remarkable history of runes, the magic they hold, and the tales that are still told about them today. We'll discover how an alphabet had such power. A power that those who used it believed the spoken word held enough power to manifest the non-physical to the physical and how a form of writing linked people with the gods and with fate. Runes are indeed remarkable, for both those who believe in magic and those who do not.

Thought to be an ancient form of writing used by the Germanic people, the runic script was used in charms, spells,

Introduction

blessings, and curses. It was also used as a fortune-telling form of divination and demarcated areas like property, burial grounds, and ceremonial lands. Scholars date this ancient language back to at least the 1st century. Some runic writings are so ancient, in fact, that they have been found in tombs that date back to before Christ. Regardless of how old the language is, runes began to gain popularity early in the 1st century and peaked before becoming mostly unused. This is not to say that the runic script is no longer in use. In fact, runes are still in use today in some regions of Scandinavia. As an alphabet and written language, runes have a complicated history. They were probably invented as a communication method unknown to the Greek and Roman empires, allowing the Germanic people to send strategic messages and stay ahead of the empire's invasions.

Originally thought to be a form of pure communication, runes were later discovered to be an embodiment of magic. Some believed a gift from Odin and the fates themselves. From as early as the 1st century (AD), the Germanic people may have begun to use runes as a written language. However, as even the word 'rune' suggests, runes hold far more significance than text alone. In Germanic (Gothic - runa), the word means secret or whisper. While in old Irish, Gaelic (rún) means mystery, secret, or intention. These meanings in themselves should give a hint to the power behind runes and as we delve deeper into the history, cultural significance, and importance of runes throughout the ages.

The poem Hávamál tells the complete legend of the god Odin who hung himself from a tree, impaled on a spear. Forbidding all other gods and mortals from helping him, he offered himself up as a sacrifice to gain the runes' knowledge. During this time, Odin focused on the fates, willing himself to gain the knowledge of the runes. On the 9th night, the runes became clear to him. Filled with the knowledge of the fates,

Introduction

Odin handed the language to his people so that they could once again be close to the gods.

Rune sagas tell fables of magical items imbued with the power of the gods by way of runic writings and carvings, giving inanimate objects and the people who yielded them enormous power. So strong was the Germanic people's belief during the Viking Age that those tales and fables of magic and runes are still told today. Notably, in Egil's Saga, the poet Egil Skallagrimsson tells of both the bad and good sides of runic magic and warns against using runic magic for the wrong reasons. Warnings against the heresy of burial and sacrificial lands were often sealed with curses. Those who tried to damage the placed runes were met with an unfortunate end, while the runes remained unharmed.

These kinds of fables and stories are hardly surprising when one delves into the history of the Germanic tribes. Their affinity for reading omens, and their relationship with nature, their gods, and their own magic. Vikings relied heavily on their intuition and nature for divination purposes. This reliance was translated to the runic script. The Vikings knew on a deeper level that magic came from within them and seemed to trust that magic to guide them on their life and spiritual journey. As time marched on, runes seemed to take more of an ownership purpose, but this was not to say that runic magic was lost entirely. Instead, it was the uprising of Christianity that forced the rune alphabet back to its original 'secret' state.

Some hid the language in fear of persecution. In contrast, others proudly carved the script on other nation's artifacts as an act of defiance. Notably, items such as staff and wands and weapons containing rune script were found among the relics of tribes outside of the Viking culture. This suggests that while the crusades were going on, many still sought to use magic, regardless of what Christianity dictated. Because runes were used hundreds of years prior, the script and magical alphabet became synonymous with an added advantage. Perhaps this was due to the runes' magic, or maybe it was the owner's belief in the runes that gave them the magic they needed to get through battles, voyages, and the claiming of land. However, the fact remains that runic is still used today, and people still believe deeply in the magic.

People have been practicing divination for centuries. It seemed only natural that runic would eventually be used for divination purposes as a way to hide this magic in plain sight. Some chose items such as crystals, tea leaves, and bones to master divination. The ancient practice of casting runes and carving charms with the script eventually evolved into a divination practice. As an oracular method, runes provided the reader with insight into their future. They allowed the reader to connect with their own magic—the magic of the universe and the fates.

While most believed that magic was only given to some, as the runic spread, the reality became apparent that magic was, in fact, a gift that everyone had. The runes were simply a way of receiving that magic and being given insight into the future. Masters of runic magic understood that divination with runes relied heavily on a person's intuition to manifest the answers they needed. More importantly, the future was malleable, and that once a person knew what their fate was, they were able to change it.

Only in the medieval ages did runic magic be understood by cultures outside of Scandinavia and Northern Germany. Tales of necromancy, healing, and divination reached the shores of countries other than those inhabited by Germanic tribes. As the Christian and Muslim churches moved to squash the upsurge of this kind of paganism, it became apparent that if organized religion feared runic magic, it was obviously powerful. In perhaps an ironic twist of fate, the church insisted on proof of this magic. Especially when they expected others to believe in a deity that was neither tangible nor provided

Introduction

evidence of its magic in the form of the miracles preached. Because of this, and because of the intense Norse occupation in some areas that runic continued to thrive side by side with Christianity. To this day, some remains of early Christian churches display runic script offering blessings. Despite the crusades' best attempts; most runic grave markings could not be eradicated entirely with Christian script.

If you are reading this book, then you are either interested in or believe in the power of magic, divination, and the runes. Like those before you believed, runic magic is not exclusive and can go hand in hand with any belief system, deity, or spiritual journey. Suppose there is anything to be learned from the frantic and dramatic history of runes. In that case, magic is deeply connected to those who practice it and those who believe it exists. While some choose to believe that magic needs to be categorized into black, gray, or white, all magic has the ability to heal or to harm. It is the intention of the rune caster that creates the magic.

In the same way, the seeker intends to determine the answers one receives when using runes for divination purposes. Intuition, pure intention, and clear, concise thoughts are essential when you finally decide to cast your runes. Being in touch with that magic, being able to immerse yourself deeply into this spiritual journey, and being open and receptive to what the fates present to you will be essential as you begin to delve into the world of runes. The ability to read this secret is within you if you choose to open the door and to believe that you are as magical as you want to be.

ONE

What Are Runes?

ORIGINALLY THOUGHT TO BE AN ANCIENT ALPHABET. THE FIRST six letters made up the palindrome Futhark. Runic remains a mystery. Used by the Germanic people, runic was a written system used for charms, spells, blessings, curses, and divination to help people find clarity in their lives. While the runic language was in place from around the 1st century, it gained extreme popularity within the last 100 years when runes' magic and spirituality became known further abroad.

Regardless of its original intended usage, the Elder Futhark runes are the oldest writing form in Northern Europe. Used for divination purposes for hundreds of years, the small stones have become synonymous with a 'magical' alphabet. Physical objects have been used for the purposes of magic since the dawn of time. Items like crystals, tea leaves, and bones were used by master diviners. These types of readings gave extremely accurate results. The ancient practice of casting runes and carving or writing charms and curses into stone and rock is no different. The ancient oracle method provides insight to readers, assisting in connecting a person's own magic to the universe, fates, or gods. The true magic of the runic alphabet is that, unlike some of its other written counterparts, runes and the magical wisdom they hold are still used today.

Runes have a complex history that is shrouded in mystery. The usage of them has never been definitively ascertained. Still, it is presumed they were more than likely developed as a way to communicate in secret. Later it was discovered that runic was a written language and had a deep connection to magic and divination. As a result, runes are still considered an embodiment of magic and a gift from the fates. In the past, it was believed that only those who were able to practice magic were given the ability to use the runes. However, as we now know, everyone has magic within them, and everyone has been given the gift to read the runes. The runes were simply a way of writing this magic or receiving the answers to the question presented to the fates. Seen as symbols of magical power and a connection to something greater than us, runes help people feel a deeper connection to their spiritual self. Runic magic relies heavily on a person's own intuition. This intuition manifests the answers or internal needs we are struggling with. In doing so, the runes can help find solutions to questions we can't answer.

The History of Runic

Also referred to as the Futhark, the runic alphabet has no definitive record of early usage. From the 1st century (AD), tribes from the Germanic, Britain, Scandinavia, and Icelandic people were writing in runes. While runic writings may have had a later start as far as written languages are concerned, they were used well into the 17th century. The most commonly believed origin theory is that the Goths created the runic alphabet and was later influenced by the Latin alphabet between the 1st and 2nd centuries (AD). Currently, scholars believe that there are three variations of the runic script. These are; Teutonic script or Germanic script. This was used as far back as 700 (AD) by the tribes who occupied Northern Europe. The Anglian script, which was used in Britain. The Nordic or Scandinavian script, which was used in Scandinavia and Iceland.

The early Germanic scripts were divided into eight letters each, were called ættir and consisted of 24 letters in total. The alphabet was named Futhark after the first six sounds these letters made; f, u, th, a, r and k. The Anglo-Saxons added four letters bringing their alphabet to 28 letters. After 900 (AD), more letters were added to bring the total to 33. Also, there were some differences in the changes to the letters, although not significant. In the Scandinavian variant, the sounds were richer. Still, instead of adding letters to the original alphabet, the Futhark script users compounded the letters so that the same letter could represent different sounds. An example of this is the script, which represents the letters k and g. This meant that the Futhark was eventually compounded to 16 letters in total for the Scandinavian alphabet.

The formation of the alphabet was completed by the early 5th century. This has become evident with the discovery and study of the Kylver stone, which has the complete Futhark and the 'p' rune.

Charms and Memorials

Carved into rock faces, trees and used as charms on pieces of wood and stone, runes have been used for divination and magic throughout the ages. Many cultures and tribes cast these symbols in the form of tiles to practice magic, foresee the future, or ask for guidance in future decisions. These runes were read by interpreting the patterns and meanings of the script. Since the dark ages, the Vikings used their runes for divination and written language and oracles and as items for protection. This was done not just to create sounds but to signify entire words or concepts of importance. Every rune has an attachment to a Norse god, and every rune has a story. These runes were divided into three groups or ættir, plus the addition of the Wyrd rune and the Fate rune. Later in this book, we will take a more in-depth look into each rune and its particular significance. Each rune has a threefold meaning and has an allocated phoneme. We'll reveal later the importance of this three-fold meaning and the magic of this script.

Runes as a Written Language

The Elder Futhark is the oldest form of runic script. While the runic alphabet has evolved and developed with time, the Elder Futhark is most commonly used, even today. Derived from the first six letters of the alphabet, the Elder Futhark became synonymous with mystery and magic. The earliest Elder Futhark runic writings have been dated back to approximately 150 AD, with later forms of runic being found in around 700 AD. By 1100 AD Northern Europe was experiencing the surge of Christianity. This upsurge placed pressure on the people who still used the ancient form of writing to convert to the Latin alphabet. Despite this, the Futhark held strong, and instead of disappearing altogether, it evolved. The Elder Futhark gave way around 700 AD to the Younger Futhark, which was used until 1100 AD. The Younger Futhark was further divided into long-branch runes and short-branch runes. Runic is still used by certain families in rural Sweden to this day.

As mentioned before, the origins of the runic alphabet are shrouded in mystery, with some believing it to be a variation of the Old Italic scripts. Other scholars have suggested influence from the Rhaetic, Venetic, Etruscan, and Old Latin alphabets. These scripts seem to have had the same letter shaping, but runic is unique in its connection to the esoteric. The mystery of runes and how the script moved from region to region is also unknown. While the oldest dated inscriptions were found in Denmark, it is presumed that the script did not originate in Denmark but was brought to the country. However, the people of Scandinavia will tell you that the runes were given to the Germanic people by Odin after he sacrificed himself to learn the script.

The Kylver stone is the first known artifact to display the Elder Futhark's completed order and the 'p' rune, which had been absent until then. While there was no written difference in the Futhark from region to region, there was a definite difference in the areas' spoken languages, which lends more to the mystery that surrounds runic. How could there be a universal written language for the region spoken by everyone when their dialects were so different? Some think that it is this very fact that earned runic its name, 'mystery.' Whatever its origins are, the runic alphabet has been used widely for longer than most alphabets and is variable in its writings. Runic can be read from left to right or right to left. Often words were not clearly divided, although some later runic writings were found to have a dot to separate words. Runes have been found on all materials and somehow have managed to survive even Christian attempts at changing gravestones to Christian writings. Runic writings have been found on cliffs, large rocks, ancient buildings, and even Christian churches. Large slabs have been found in presumed burial grounds not only to mark graves but to warn against the desecration of the ground. Many magical inscriptions, including prayers, curses, and charms, have been found on pieces of jewelry, weapons, and even farming tools. Later, runes were found to mark areas of trade, law enforcement, and politics.

To date, four runic alphabets and their short-branch or long-branch forms have been discovered. There is strong speculation that with runic still in use today, there are many more versions that remain a secret.

Runes Through Historical Culture

Although the exact dates are difficult to pinpoint due to conflicting scholarly research, it seems the Elder Futhark script came into use from at least 160 AD. The Elder form of the script was used until 700 AD. the Younger Futhark was used until around 1100 AD, and the Medieval Futhorc until much later. It is thought that the script was designed to be carved into metal and wood. Still, during the age of the Vikings, large runestones were used throughout Scandinavia. With the exact use of runestones still up in the air, scholars can agree that they are critical to studying this historical period. They have given a tremendous amount of insight into where the Germanic people traveled and have been found as far abroad as England, Central Europe, and the historic Roman city of Constantinople.

As mentioned before, by 700 AD, the use of the Elder Futhark had become prominent. They began to evolve at this stage, reducing their character value and becoming the Younger Futhark throughout Scandinavia, and the Anglo-Saxon / Medieval Futhorc, which will be discussed further in Chapter 2 throughout Britain and Frisia. While it is relatively easy to track the evolution of the runic alphabet, the origins are still a point of debate. For students and scholars of runic, the standard theory is that the Elder Futhark was a variant of the Greek and Roman alphabets. Still, for believers in the practice of magic, Odin bestowed the Futhark's knowledge to people.

What is known with certainty is that right from the outset of the writing system's usage, variations, often small but noticeable, were present in the script. What is of particular interest is that although there were several Germanic tribes and languages, the Elder Futhark, for the most part, had the same letter meanings and pronunciation of the corresponding words throughout the various dialects. While the sounds would've almost certainly been slightly different, as a written text, the Elder Futhark was a universal language. Written for a common purpose so that all tribes who were educated in it could understand what was written.

As the forefather of all other runic scripts, the Elder Futhark was found on artifacts dating back to the 1st century. These runic writings have been found throughout the Germanic occupied territories but no further abroad than the Northern Germanic regions at first. This area's runic artifacts have been found in Scandinavia, Germany, and Eastern Europe. Later, dated items were found in England, the Netherlands, and Southern Germany. Still, for now, there is no evidence that the Elder Futhark was used any further abroad. The runic script found from the Northern Germanic territories was primarily used to represent property ownership and occasionally would include curses or charms. Because of this, most believe that there was no real function to the Elder Futhark until much later in its use. Having said that, scholars of magic believe that the script was almost certainly used for divination and magical purposes during that time.

From around 700 AD, the Younger Futhark came into play and led the runic script's uprising. Consisting of fewer characters and simplified to a certain extent, the Younger Futhark became commonly used throughout Scandinavia. While the Elder Futhark seemed to have been a more exclusive script used by only a few Germanic tribes, far more people used the Younger version. Due to the speed at which the newer version of the Futhark spread throughout Scandinavia and Eastern Europe, there has been some speculation that it was perhaps taught for and with a purpose. However, there has been no evidence of a specific authority driving its spread and usage.

What is interesting about the Younger Futhark is that the script, although uniform and not as changeable as the Elder Futhark, did have regional variations. In Norway, the long-branch version of runic was far more prevalent, while in Denmark and Sweden, the short-twig versions of the script were used. What is more clear to historians is how and why the Younger Futhark spread throughout various areas. During its uprising, the Viking Age of Scandinavia was at its pinnacle. Because of this, runestones and runic artifacts have been found throughout Europe and began to make their way to the shores of Britain and Frisia. Considering that its spread was when Christianity was on the rise and Vikings were seen as heathens, the prevalence of runic writings speaks volumes for its popularity. Runestones and artifacts that contained the script from this Viking Age era were used to commemorate the dead. Mark ownership, tell tales of battles against the Christian crusades and be used for curses and charms. Through this battle against Christianity and the Vikings' movement to gain territory, the Younger Futhark landed on Britain's shores. It once again underwent a transformation to the Anglo-Saxon Futhorc.

The Anglo-Saxon Futhorc went in the opposite direction of the Younger Futhark. It added elaborate sounds and letters to the runic alphabet. Prevalent in Britain and the Netherlands (Frisia), it seems as if the Anglo-Saxon Futhorc began to be used from the 5th century. This version had in common with its forefather, the Elder Futhark, that the script was quite varied. As a written alphabet, the Anglo-Saxon Futhorc was used to write the spoken languages of Old English and Old Frisian. With Christianity as a driving force, the script was more of a secret language. Today, less than 200 known inscriptions of Anglo-Saxon Futhorc exist. There are some instances where coins, weapons, and crosses were found with these types of inscriptions. For the most part, they were overwritten with Christian text in the form of the Latin alphabet. Some churches still have the Anglo-Saxon Futhorc inscribed into doors, perhaps as a way to try to convert people from paganism to Christianity. Clergy manuscripts used the Futhorc and Latin scripts side by side.

By the 10th century AD, a new version of the Younger Futhark began to emerge throughout Scandinavia. By 1200 AD, the Younger Futhark had once again evolved to the Medieval Futhorc. The changes were not dramatic, though, with the shape of some of the dots changed to accommodate certain sounds. These did not count as new runic letters but were partnered alongside the sound made when pronouncing the old rune. Perhaps the most notable change was how the Medieval Futhorc runes were read. Doubling some consonant sounds and binding runes together to fall in line with their Latin counterpart. An example of this would be the 't' rune, which represented the 'th' sound. In the Medieval Futhorc, 'th' would be differentiated from t by a dot.

Today, a form of runic is still used in Dalarna, a province in Sweden. Unlike the Futhark of the past, not much evolution has occurred. The script remains mostly unchanged from the 16th century to today's form of Dalrune. Runic has shown itself to be a tenacious form of writing. To this day, it is used in modern-day pagan, divination, and magical practices. The runic script has been adapted to appear in classic fantasy novels and films, keeping the mystery of this written language alive.

Runes and Magic

The Nords believed that the god Odin hung himself from a tree for nine days and nights as a form of sacrifice to gain the runes' knowledge. So great was this knowledge that Odin felt he needed to share it with others. As such, this information was imparted to human beings to bring people closer to the gods and the fates. When delving into runes, it does not take long before stories of magic and castings surface. Runic magic is a way to see the future, to create charms, and to cast curses.

It is an intimately woven tapestry of fact and fiction throughout the Viking Age.

Runic sagas tell tales of magical items that held power. With the help of these inscriptions, a person could look into their future, prevent misfortune, and impart magical qualities into inanimate objects. Such was the belief of those who held onto runic magic that curses, spells, and conjurings were often written in runic. While it is true that some inscriptions have been found with nothing more than an ownership message, the fact remains that a great many runic finds have included at least an insinuation of magic.

Throughout the Viking Age, tales were told and are still told to this day how runes and magical words were used to heal and curse. In Skallagrimsson's saga, Egil used runes to cure a girl who had been cursed with evil runic magic. Egil carves a new set of runes, enchanting them with healing magic. These runes were put under the girl's pillow, and the child was healed. From this fable, one can ascertain that runic magic is powerful and can be extremely dangerous when used for the wrong intentions.

It wasn't long before these Nordic tales, causes, and warnings reached crusaders on a quest to spread the word of Christianity. Stories spread like wildfire of Christian crusaders attempting to overturn these stones, only to be met with an untimely ending while the stones and grounds they protected remain unharmed. The Vikings believed strongly in their gods and the omens sent to them via the fates and gods. Omens such as a flock of birds or a spooked galloping horse were taken seriously, often telling those who observed them what was to come. Because of their ability to read and how they remained in tune with nature, the Vikings kept the magic of runes strong throughout the years.

Magic and nature have always gone hand in hand, and the Vikings seemed to know this on a level that allowed them to tap into their magic earlier than most. During the medieval ages, Viking runes began to morph somewhat. More and more runes were found that hinted at an ownership purpose. This is not to say that runic magic was forgotten. In fact, it seemed to become more prevalent as tumultuous territory wars waged. Still, the magic became a little more hidden out of fear of persecution by the Christian crusaders. During this era, numerous artifacts were found that paid homage to a specific god. Runic staff and wands found that the tribes and people of that time relied heavily on magic when going to battle or requesting protection or abundance in otherwise uncertain times.

To this day, runes and runic magic are practiced in the rural areas of Denmark, a testament to the tenacity of the runic script and the power of the magic it holds. Despite Christianity and the Viking lands' attempted occupation, runic and its magic have survived and is as powerful today as it was at its peak. The beauty of runic magic requires no particular skill and enhances a person's own intuition and inner magic. It is a guide—a means by which to reconnect a person to their spirituality and gain access to the intuitive knowledge they already possess but cannot otherwise access.

TWO

Runes Lore

THE ANCIENT RUNIC ALPHABET AND THE LORE SURROUNDING IT are rich and deep, being traced back to the 1st century. Studied today by linguistics and orthographers the world over, the Elder Futhark and its evolved variations are steeped in traditions still practiced today. However, the how or why of runes does not matter to those who follow these ancient writings and their power.

As one delves deeper into the lore, it becomes apparent that the rise of Christianity had a massive influence on the supposed reasons for the evolution of runic inscriptions and writings. While scholars of these ancient writings will try hard to convince people that runic writings were nothing more than memorials, practical information, or graffiti written by ancient tribes, the contents of some of the artifacts cannot be ignored. These artifacts reflect a long tradition of magic and myth and show the strong relationship the runic people had with the gods, fate, and magic. This is particularly evident where large rocks used to mark ceremonial or burial grounds were inscribed with warning curses to prevent an area's destruction. Runic was inscribed on jewelry and on weaponry, which protected its wearer or invoked the gods' strength to the wielder in battle. Simple farming tools were often inscribed with runic chants, wishing the farmer a good harvest and reminding them to be thankful for the melting snow.

According to Norse legends, Odin became jealous of the Norns, three women who created all beings' fates. The Norns would shape futures by carving runes into Yggdrasil's tree; this allowed these fates to filter through to the Nine Worlds. While sitting on his throne in Asgard, Odin became increasingly envious of the Norns' power and wisdom. He set out to prove himself worthy enough to read the runes. He pierced himself with his own spear and forbade the other gods from helping him. While in limbo between death and life, the runes began to appear to Odin, making him one of the wisest and most revered entities in the cosmos. Through this sacrifice, human beings were given the gift of the runes as a way to impart that knowledge and communicate with the gods. This legend in itself hints at the enormous power that runes yield, not just as a connection to the gods but to the runic script's connection to fate. Runes have always been an interwoven tapestry of legend, magic, and practicality, which has not changed over time and will unlikely ever change.

The Elder Futhark

The oldest form of the runic alphabet, Elder Futhark, was a written system used by various tribes during the migration period. While its exact formation date is still a topic of debate, it is widely believed that the Futhark as we know it today came into being between the 1st and 2nd centuries. This has been backed by artifacts that have runic inscriptions on them. These artifacts include not only the now-famous runestones but jewelry, pottery, weapons, and rudimentary tools. As newer dialects came into play through the ages, the Elder Futhark became a forgotten language until 1865 when a

Norwegian scholar of runic inscriptions deciphered and reignited this ancient language.

Like its date of formation, the Elder Futhark's written origins are also uncertain. Some believe that it was derived from Old Italic scripts, while others believe it comes from the Latin alphabet. Until the 19th century, many scholars believed it to be a variation of the Greek alphabet. The age of some artifacts later discredited this theory as the Greeks and Goths historically only came into contact with each other later in history. Whatever its origins, the script was eventually credited to a group of people who had been immersed in the Roman culture. The Elder Futhark was almost certainly created as a means of written communication between a specific group of people who did not want outside tribes to know what they were saying. Whether inscriptions were used for magical or practical purposes only came to light much later, with some runes being translated as curses, instructions, or brief memoirs.

The Elder Futhark of 24 runes is broken into symbols, with each symbol representing the rune's sound. Later versions of the script amended, added, or took away runes for their specific purpose. We'll look at these in detail later. What is interesting about these runes is that besides the sound value, each rune has a literal meaning as well as an esoteric tie. Runes such as Teiwaz and Ansuz were thought to invoke specific gods and were sometimes used on weapons or farming or harvest tools. Because of this, it is doubtful that the runic alphabet was used only for written language and infers that it was used in conjunction with esoteric and mythological functions.

The Anglo-Saxon Futhorc

The Anglo-Saxon runes, derived from the first six runes, are known as the Futhorc and were used by the Anglo-Saxons from around the 5th century onwards. Derived from the 24 symbol Elder Futhark, the Futhorc runes consisted of 29 runes, which were later expanded to 33. By the 11th century, runes were rarely used and were replaced by the Old English Latin alphabet. This, however, did not stop some groups from continuing to use their ancient language. The earliest Futhorc was almost precisely the same as the Elder Futhark except for a split in some runes, which increased its total number.

There are several theories as to how the Anglo-Saxon Futhorc came into being. Some believe that the script was adjusted and developed in Frisia after coming into contact with Germanic and Scandinavia tribes. The script was later carried to Britain. Others believe that the Futhorc originated in Britain and was last modified before ending up in Frisia. However, these theories are purely speculative as there is not enough archeological or historical evidence to support either.

As we mentioned above, other than a split in some letters, the Futhorc and Futharks were nearly identical, but this changed when the runic language landed in England. Taking influence from Latin scriptoria and heavily influenced by the surge of Anglo-Saxon Christianity, the Futhorc expanded. This is especially evident around the 7th century, when Christianization began to outlaw paganism and its associated scripts. Sadly, this movement also resulted in the destruction of five centuries worth of artifacts. As a result, less than 200 Anglo-Saxon Futhorc runes exist today. This destruction did not destroy evidence of magic, which has further cemented popular opinion that the language was primarily used for divination and esoteric purposes. Symbols have been found on sword pommels, other weapons, bones, stone crosses, and items which later became known as 'Futhorc rings.' It is believed that runic stones and trinkets can still be found along the East Coast of Southern England and West Frisia.

Younger Futhark

Found throughout the Viking settlements and Scandinavia, the Younger Futhark was used from the 9th century. The Elder Futhark seemed to be available only to a very elite few people who used it. Today only about 350 Elder Futhark inscriptions have survived while more than 3,000 Younger Futhark runestones still exist. This is because of the period and because the Younger Futhark seems to have been spread wider through Scandinavia and was used for everything from casual notes to magic, curses, and instructions. What is noteworthy, though, is that inscriptions used for magical purposes seemed to use a mixture of both the Younger and Elder Futhark, with the Elder being used to encrypt the text.

Near the 9th century, the Younger Futhark was reduced from 24 runes to 16 runes. This meant that some consonants were no longer used in the script. While there is still some speculation as to the order in which the Futhark was shortened, it is clear that the dialect changes were to suit various tribes and regions. Most notably, these changes were the long-branch (Danish) version and the short-branch or twig (Swedish and Norwegian) rune versions. Most believe that these branches of the Futhark were evolved for functional purposes only. The long-branch versions were used to inscribe on stone, and the short-twig version was used for wood or softer inscription materials.

Danish or Long-Branch Runes

Derived from the Younger Futhark, the Danish or long-branch runes were reduced from 24 runes to 16 runes as the alphabet evolved through the ages. The long-branch runes became synonymous with Denmark, where inscriptions were primarily etched into stone instead of wood or softer inscription materials.

ᛓ - Fehu (Fé); wealth or cattle

ᚾ - Uruz (Ûr); iron or rain

Þ - Thurs (Purisaz); giant
ᚨ - Ansuz (Ass); the Gods or estuary
ᚱ - Raido (Raidõ); ride
ᚲ - Kaunan (Kauna); ulcer or boil
ᚼ - Haglaz (Hag(a)laz); hail
ᚾ - Naudiz (Nauder); need, threat or emergency
I - Isaz (Isa); ice
ᛄ - Jeran (Jêra/Ar); plenty, year, or a good harvest
ᚼ - Sowilo (Sõwilõ / Sol); the sun
↑ - Tiwaz (Té²waz / Tyr); the god Tyr
ᛒ - Berkanan (Bjork / Bjarkan); birch tree
ᛉ - Mannaz (Maor); man or person
ᛚ - Laguz (Laukaz / Logr); sea, lake or body of water
ᛘ - Algiz / Yr (Algiz); yew tree or elm tree

Rök or Short-Branch Runes

The Rök or short-branch runes were also a variation of the Younger Futhark. They were particularly prevalent throughout the Swedish and Norwegian areas. The original Younger Futhark was amended to make inscriptions on wood and softer materials more manageable and quicker for the writer.

ᚠ - Fehu (Fé); wealth
ᚢ - Uruz (Ûr); iron or rain
Þ - Thurs (Purisaz); giant
ᚨ - Ansuz (Ansuz); the Gods
ᚱ - Raido (Raidõ); ride
ᚲ - Kaunan (Kauna); ulcer
ᚼ - Haglaz (Hag(a)laz); hail
ᚾ - Naudiz (Naudiz); need
I - Isaz (Isaz); ice
ᛄ - Jeran (Jêra); plenty
' - Sowilo (Sõwilõ); the sun
↑ - Tiwaz (Té²waz); the god Tyr
ᛒ - Berkanan (Berkanan); birch tree
ᛉ - Mannaz (Mannaz); man

ᛚ - Laguz (Laukaz); sea
ᛁ - Algiz (Algiz); yew tree

Hälsinge or Staveless Runes

Known as the Staveless runes, the Hälsingland runes are named after runestones discovered in Hälsingland, Sweden. These runes are characterized by the lack of staves (vertical marks) on specific letters. While most of the letters are without these marks, this is not true for the symbols representing Fehu, Thurs, Kaunan (Kenaz), and Sowilo, where partial or entire staves are present. While these runes are prevalent in Hälsingland, they are not exclusive to the area, with Staveless runes found in Medelpad, Södermanland, and Bergen.

For many years, there wasn't a difference between the Younger Futhark and the Hälsingland runes. Still, with further study, it became apparent that the lack of staves was particularly evident in some letters. The reason for the evolution of these runes is still hotly contested today. Popular thought is that the lack of staves is a result of the carving material used.

The Medieval Runes

The Futhorc evolved from the Younger Futhark and was primarily different from the introduction of the dot. Used from the 13th century to the 16th century, the medieval runes were used in competition with the Latin Alphabet. While most believed that the Latin alphabet would replace the Futhorc runes, it is very apparent that the Latin alphabet was mostly used by the elite and the clergy while the Futhorc continued to thrive among the tribes. With the rise of Christianity, one would think that the chosen Latin alphabet would've been exclusively used by the church. Some artifacts such as bells, ironwork on doors, and church walls still have the Futhorc remnants. What is still not understood is whether these were for esoteric or protective purposes with Christianity in its birth phases or whether this was purely a form of communication to lure people to the church for conversion.

Regardless of its usage, the Futhorc has been recognized

as a substantial modification of the Younger Futhark. It can only be presumed that it was easier to modify the script rather than learn an entirely new alphabet. The Futhorc was so popular that the Latin alphabet borrowed the 'p' rune to add to its own alphabet.

ᚠ - feoh; wealth
ᚢ - ūr; aurochs
ᚦ - þorn; thorn
ᚩ - ōs; one of the gods or mouth
ᚱ - rād; ride
ᚳ - cēn; torch
X - gyfu; gift
ᚹ - pynn; mirth
ᚺ - hægl; hail
ᛏ - nȳd; need
ᛁ - īs; ice
ᛄ - gēr; year or harvest
ᛇ - ēoh; yew
ᛈ - peorð; unknown or perhaps pear tree
ᛉ - eolh; elk sedge
ᛋ - sigel; the sun
ᛏ - Tīp; glory
ᛒ - beorc; birch
ᛖ - eh; horse
ᛗ - mann; man
ᛚ - lagu; lake
ᛝ - Ing; hero
ᛟ - ēðel; inherited estate
ᛞ - dæg; day
ᚪ - āc; oak
ᚫ - æsc; ash tree
ᚣ - ȳr; bow
ᛡ - īor; eel
ᛠ - ēar; grave

The Dalecarlian Runes

Known as the Dalrunes, the Dalecarlian runes are the most extended surviving runic script used in Dalarna until the 20th century. The local tribes in this Swedish province wrote or carved their names in the runic script on everything from bowls to cornerstones and walls. Because of this, it is thought that other regions and areas in Scandinavia may still use this form of runic script, continuing the tradition of it being 'secret.'

As a derivation of medieval runes, the Dalrunes are a combination of the Futhorc and the Latin alphabet. However, as time has passed, it seemed that more and more letters were replaced by Latin lettering. The runic alphabet was converted almost entirely into a particular version of amalgamated lettering. While runic writings are an ancient tradition in themselves, Dalrunes date back only to the 16th century. With them still being used today, many speculate whether runic writings were learned as part of family traditions or if they were a learned subject exclusive to specific tribes and families.

THREE

Rune Meanings
_____

Craftsmen and the owners of runes inscribed their names onto ancient runes. Still, many ancient runes remain anonymous with no apparent owners or purpose. Because of this, many believe that runes and runic writings were not just used to write but as charms and tools in magic. Some will claim that there is no evidence that runes were used for divination purposes. Still, with its name literally meaning 'secret,' 'whisper,' or 'something hidden,' it is difficult to believe that runes weren't used for esoteric purposes.

The 6th-century Björketorp runestone strongly implies the runes esoteric powers with the one side loosely translated into English, saying, 'I foresee perdition,' or 'I foresee prediction.' The other side states, 'I, master of the runes conceal here runes of power. Incessantly (plagued by) maleficence, (doomed to) insidious death (is) he who breaks this (monument).' Many have stated that those who have tried to move the mammoth stone were met with insidious and untimely deaths as part of a grave field. Always with the stone and its surrounding menhirs remaining untouched.

Similarly, the Stentoften and Istaby runestones have a curse inscribed on them and directly refer to animal sacrifices, which were often performed for fertility purposes around the inscription time. The inscriptions as translated in English, read, 'To the dwellers (and) guests Haþuwulfar gave full year, Hariwulfar ... ... I, master of the runes conceal here nine bucks, nine stallions, Haþuwulfar gave fruitful year, Hariwulfar ... ... I, master of the runes conceal here runes of power. Incessantly (plagued by) maleficence, (doomed to) insidious death (is) he who this breaks.'

While scholars and skeptics alike may regard these inscriptions as nothing more than a 'trespassers beware' sign, the fact remains that no sign is put up without just reason and, for the most part, is placed to warn people of prospective or impending danger. However, the fact remains that centuries later, people still believe in mysticism and power, not only of runic curses but of runic magic.

Modern practitioners of runic magic will tell you that knowing how to read your runes and respecting the information given to you will unlock personal growth and insight into your past, present, and future. Becoming emotionally and physically in tune with your runes is important, knowing how to read them. Some people may opt to buy their runes, while others choose to make them, preferring each rune's intimate carving. It is important to note that rune divination is not a way of telling your own or someone else's fortune. It is a tool for guidance and helps you in the potential outcomes as a message from the gods or fate. Reading your runes can be tricky, though, with answers often being obscure. Thus, it is necessary to ask a specific question to get a pertinent answer. After all, one does not ask for salt when they are actually thirsty. Your runes cannot give you exact answers or specific details. Still, they can assist you in continuing or altering the path you are on.

Runes and Their Meanings

Before Christianity, the spoken and written word were powerful tools in manifesting magic. When one pronounced a word, it would be with a specific meaning in mind. Once a sentence was spoken, it could never be taken back, as if the word and the pronunciation of that word manifested it into something physical. For pre-Christian Vikings specifically, words created their reality.

When the Vikings people carved runes into objects, it was with a specific purpose in mind. The intention was always to alter their reality in some way, shape, or form. What is important is that they realized that their existence may not have been changed in an absolute way. Instead, they would be equipped with the knowledge to alter that reality. How this was done was incredibly well thought out, especially for that era. The runic alphabet assigns a visual, physical object to each of its phonemes. Beyond that, each rune has a threefold meaning; the physical, the letter, and the esoteric. In this way, one can form words, physically manifest what they desire, or tap into the supernatural through divination.

Today's scholars have long forgotten the significance between this relationship of sound/word and the physical object; they tend to think that these objects or physical representations are entirely arbitrary. The reality is that the Northern Germanic people intended to be a strong connection between all three representations of the script. For example, if we take the word 'thorn,' the word needs to be broken down into its specific phonemes for its hidden message to be deciphered. The phoneme th, o, r, and n would each mean something, so the word thorn suddenly becomes a message that means something entirely different. The meaning of the rune is the primary message given to the rune reader.

The Norse people believe so strongly in Odin's story. His sacrifice to obtain the runic script that they simply could not and still cannot think that the lettering is entirely random. Therefore, the relationship between the sound made, the word read, the esoteric meaning, and the rune's physical representation are all interwoven and inherently meaningful to the writer, reader, or caster.

Runes were never meant to be solely a means to communicate in a written language. They were meant to be tools that had a deep meaning connecting the physical to the metaphysical. It was a way for human beings to communicate with the fates and tap into their intuition and their own magic. Sure, there have been stories of 'black magic,' where runes were used for necromancy and curses. This, although off-putting to some, is a testament to the power of runic magic and its ability to redirect a person's fate. This was the central focus of runic magic—the ability to change or shift the future. Its intention was not to harm but to protect and offer guidance when the Norse people felt the gods had turned against people.

These fables and stories are not all dark or black magic, though. There have been tales of healing and powerful masters of runic magic scraping off curses and writing over the cursed object to heal the person or the cursed place. For the most part, runes and runic script warn of curses to prevent sacred and sacrificial grounds from being damaged. They are memorials to the dead and well wishes for the spirits of those entering Valhalla. They are tokens of thanks or inscriptions of possession to show that the original reader's physical manifestation came into being by merely requesting it and changing the course of their fate. Runes are a tool to unlock your magic, give you insight, and aid you on your spiritual and life journey. The words are essential, the meanings are more important, and your intentions are of utmost importance. Respect the magic, and it will respect you.

Fehu

Represented as ᚠ and pronounced 'fay-who,' the symbol has a literal translation to 'cattle.' When seeking the more profound meaning, Fehu's symbolism refers to new beginnings, wealth, success, emotional security, and abundance in your life and fertility.
Esoteric symbolism - New beginnings, wealth, and property.

Uruz

Written as ᚁ, and verbalized as 'ooo-rooze,' this is the symbol for the bull. Uruz symbolizes untapped or untamed potential, inner strength and tenacity, courage, and freedom. It signifies a time for growth and beginning on a new path in life.
Esoteric symbolism - Manifestation and endurance.

Thurisaz

Represented as ᚦ and pronounced 'thoor-ee-saws,' Thurisaz is a rune of protection. It warns against potential threats and dishonesty to achieve an objective. Literally meaning 'giants' and referencing Thor and Loki, Thurisaz represents destructive forces, whether they be natural, physical, or spiritual.
Esoteric symbolism - Resistance and strength.

Ansuz

Ansuz is symbolized as ᚫ and is verbalized as 'awn-sooze.' It literally means 'mouth of God,' and interpreted explicitly as 'Odin.' Ansuz is particularly significant as it symbolized an old connection to the gods and infers divine wisdom and a direct

link of this wisdom to the gods. Ansuz is often connected to creativity, persuasion, and communications.
Esoteric symbolism - The sovereign god, or breath.

Raiho

With its literal meaning as 'ride' or 'wagon,' and its symbol being R, Raiho is pronounced 'rye-though.' Placing emphasis on the journey of life, and not becoming hung up on the obstacles or stops along the way, Raiho reminds the receiver of fate's role in their life, the effects of outside influences, and the understanding of acceptance in events outside of the control of one's life.
Esoteric symbolism - Journey.

Kenaz

Symbolized as <, Kenaz is pronounced 'kane-nawze,' and Kenaz's literal meaning is 'torch.' On a deeper level, Kenaz is the rune of the night and represents knowledge, inspiration, and a quest to seek deeper intellect. Representing the female energy as fire, Kenaz is a powerful tool for meditation.
Esoteric symbolism - Knowledge.

Gebo

Gebo is represented by an X and is still used today as the representation of a kiss. Literally meaning 'gift,' and pronounced 'gay-boo,' Gebo symbolizes the balance between giving and receiving. This extends to both physical and emotional reciprocation and depicts how the act of giving and receiving strengthens relationships between people, the universe, and the gods.

Esoteric symbolism - Fairtrade, marriage, or sacrifice.

Wunjo

Wunjo is represented by the symbol P or p, and is verbalized as 'woon-yo.' Literally, Wunjo means 'joy' and is a positive rune that symbolizes new beginnings be filled with joy, whether that be a new relationship or partnership. Wunjo highlights the importance of companionship through life and reminds the reader that it is essential to put joy out into the universe to receive joy back.

Esoteric symbolism - Harmony, perfection, and hope.

Hagalaz

Pronounced 'haw-gaw-laws,' and represented by the symbol H, Hagalaz literally means 'hail,' and it signifies destruction and the resulting transformation. While Hagalaz may seem to be negative, it directs one to rebirth and resilience after destruction. It reminds the reader that just because they have no control over the destruction that may occur in their lives, a new beginning and rebirth can occur. It asks the reader to confront negative behaviors and patterns to create a new beginning for themselves.

Esoteric symbolism - Massive change or crisis.

Nauthiz

Literally meaning 'need fire,' Nauthiz or Naudhiz is written as the symbol ↑ and is seen as a negative symbol. Pronounced' now-these,' Nauthiz seeks to highlight an imbalance in one's life and reminds the reader to remain patient and focused on their long-term goals. Nauthiz is sometimes seen as the

predictor of poverty, and as it brings to the forefront a need or must-have. It reminds the reader that material possessions do not necessarily bring happiness or joy.
Esoteric symbolism - Constraints or friction.

Isa

Isa is written as ⌶ and is pronounced 'ih-z-ah. Its literal meaning is 'ice,' and it symbolizes stagnation or stasis. While it may seem that Isa is negative in its meaning, it reminds the reader that even in areas where ice completely covers the ground, there is continuous preparation for growth to occur. Associated with feminine energy, Isa is seen as a symbol of underlying creativity.
Esoteric symbolism - Stillness or being static.

Jera

Pronounced 'yehr-ah' and literally translated to 'harvest' or 'year,' it is written as ᛃ. Jera represents patience and hard work and reaping the benefits of those actions. While the harvest may bring subtle changes in one's life, it means good tidings and the end of the harshness of the sowing season, reaping the reward of your hard work.
Esoteric symbolism - Harvest or reap.

Eihwaz

The written symbol ᛇ literally translates to 'yew tree' and symbolizes dualities. The Yew tree dies and transforms over time, and in this way, Eihwaz seeks to show the reader that death is both an ending and a new beginning. Pronounced' eye-warz,' the symbol is one of enlightenment, wisdom, and knowledge.
Esoteric symbolism - Kundalini and Yggdrasil.

Pertho

Written as ᛈ, Pertho's literal meaning is unknown. Sometimes referred to as a 'vessel which can be filled,' Pertho represents chance, mystery, and fertility. Otherwise known as 'potluck,' Pertho represents the powerful force of fate at work and is associated with randomness, luck, or coincidence. Arguably one of the most mysterious runes, Pertho has been a hot topic of debate amongst rune readers for years.

Esoteric symbolism - Fate.

Algiz

Algiz is verbalized as 'all-yeeze,' and literally means 'elk.' Written as the symbol ᛉ, Algiz represents the divine consciousness and spiritual awareness and protection. Algiz references the Yggdrasil (Tree of the World) and the four elk who feed off the Norse mythology tree. Algiz symbolizes that the reader receives protection from the universe and gods and that the message's receiver should be open to its guidance.

Esoteric symbolism: One's higher self and protection.

Sowilo

Literally meaning 'sun,' Sowilo is pronounced 'soe-wee-low.' The rune is written as ᛊ, or ᛋ, and represents the extreme power of the sun. The ultimate sign of positive energy, Sowilo recognizes victory and success and is a reminder that achieving success does not necessarily mean that one needs to stop seeking new success.

Esoteric symbolism - Success and wholeness.

Tiwaz

The literal meaning for the rune Tiwaz is 'the god, Tyr,' and the symbol is written as ↑. Tyr is the god of justice and law. As such, the symbol is the representation of warriors, righteousness, and honor. Tiwaz, pronounced 'tea-waz,' symbolizes self-sacrifice or sacrifice for the greater good.
Esoteric symbolism - Sacrifice and justice.

Berkana

Written as ᛒ, Berkana is sometimes referred to as Berkanan. Literally meaning 'birch tree,' Berkana is a powerful symbol of femininity and fertility. Because the birch tree is the first to grow after ice melts, it refers to motherhood, new beginnings, unconditional love, and trust. Pronounced' ber-kah-nah,' this rune is often referred to as the mother rune that carries all mankind.
Esoteric symbolism - Sanctuary and birth.

Ehwaz

Pronounced' ay-woh,' Ehwaz's literal meaning is 'horse.' In times gone by, Ehwaz, written as ᛖ symbolized forward movement. Because of the importance horses played in people's everyday lives both in status and as a mode of transport, Ehwaz represents forward-moving energy, movement, and absolute potential.
Esoteric symbolism - Trust.

Mannaz

Written as ᛗ, Mannaz has a literal meaning of 'man.' Representing humanity and mankind, Mannaz is a masculine rune with dual meanings. As an individual, Mannaz represents family, unity, and friends, and the bond that unites these groups. From a communal point of view, Mannaz, which is pronounced 'mah-naz,' helps the reader analyze challenges to solve problems and move forward.

Esoteric symbolism - Awareness and connection to humankind.

Laguz

Pronounced' log-uhz,' and written λ, Laguz is connected to a deep level with water. As a symbol of love, travel, and water, it represents nourishment and endless possibilities. Because the ocean is seen as both something to be feared and as a place of adventure and future (possibilities?) in Norse mythology, Laguz also has dual meanings. It could signify deep insecurities or fears that the reader needs to overcome.

Esoteric symbolism - Unconscious and conscious memories.

Ingwaz

Meaning 'seed' or 'the god, Ing,' Ingwaz may be written as ᛟ or °. The god Ing united the Vikings and Jutland people, creating unity. Pronounced' ing-guz,' this rune symbolizes deep romantic love, unity, sexuality, and the embodiment of a happy home, happy heart.

Esoteric symbolism - Space or process.

Dagaz

Meaning 'day' or 'new dawn,' Dagaz is pronounced 'day-gahz.' Symbolized by ᛞ, it is a positive sign. Representing mental illumination or 'seeing the light' after a dark time in one's life, Dagaz is the balance between dark and light.

Esoteric symbolism - Awakening.

Othala

As the rune of the clan lands, Othala is represented by ᛟ. This rune is associated with generational wealth, physical property, and achievement after a long journey. Othala is the final rune in the alphabetic sequence. Pronounced' oh-thall-ah,' it literally means ancestral land or homeland. Still, it is often associated with generational wisdom and spiritual power.

Esoteric symbolism - nobility, estate, and inheritance.

Wyrd

The rune Wyrd is the amalgamation of all runes, and as such, represents all things, past, present, and future. Known as Odin's rune, Wyrd is a direct reminder that all things are interconnected for all time, and that fate is always at play.

Esoteric symbolism - Fate, connectivity, and all-powerful.

FOUR

Divination With Runes

DIVINATION IS THE PROCESS IN WHICH A PERSON SETS OUT TO understand the significance or the cause of events in their life. Divination has been practiced throughout the world in modern and ancient times. In more modern times, tarot cards, astrology, and horoscopes are all forms of divination. In runic magic, the Vikings believed that divination was a manner to gain information and find out the will of the gods or fates. As time and magic evolved, it became apparent that divination was not only about the fates but also a way in which to change the future. Although almost extinct in the modern world, divination continues to be an essential part of some cultures.

Why is divination such an important part of these cultures? To understand the why, we need to first delve into the history and purpose of divination through the ages. Those who use divination do so to find solutions to problems or questions in their lives. All forms of divination rely heavily on a person's intuition, not just for the caster but for the reader or receiver. The tools that are used to practice divination are as important. They allow a person to access the energy required to receive these messages. Ancient practices of reading tea leaves, sticks, shells, bones, crystal balls, and runes were divination forms. The clarity of the answers received was thought to depend on how masterful the diviner was.

Runic magic, however, did not only have master practitioners but sought to teach everyone the power of divination. Accessing the fates and answers to questions was open to everyone. This, of course, came with separate issues with master diviners knowing that purity of intention was important. Common practitioners, sometimes accidentally and sometimes intentionally, practiced with malicious intentions. These evil intentions often led to unclear answers being given or a person going against fate's intentions.

Divination in modern times can be tricky, though. Our lives have become so complicated and frenetic, where being distracted and multitasking is common practice. This is never a good idea when choosing to use or handle your runes. The information received would be, at best, watered down, or, at worst, completely irrelevant. In those moments, it is easy for the diviner to doubt the information given to them and will begin to influence the answers received, rendering the information from the fates completely useless. Because divining is very, very rarely absolute, your tools are important, and your influence on them is extremely relevant. Remember that the energy you give to your tools is the energy your tools will give back to you. Below, we have highlighted some cleansing rituals for yourself and your runes. However, the most useful cleansing ritual is abstinence from divination and magic when you are not in the right frame of mind. An open, intuitive, and clear mind will give you everything you need to communicate with the fates. A closed, distracted, and angry mind will have your answers denied by the fates.

Reading Your Runes

Now that you trust your intuition and your ability to become involved in divination, you can begin to perform your own runic readings. Further, in this book, we have outlined some basic rune patterns and how to read them. These patterns and readings will give you the information that you seek. Remember, this information may not be immediately apparent, so keeping a rune reading diary. Record the date, question, and reading answer may be a good idea when you first start out on your divination journey.

Each rune holds a threefold message, and you must look at all of these messages when reading your runes. Keep in mind that runic is not just an alphabet; it is a divine script that connects this world to the spiritual world. Your runes allow you to tap into your intuition on a deeper level, tapping into the energy of the fates. When done correctly, divination helps you understand yourself on a deeper level and uses your intuition to communicate and connect your magic with that of the fates.

Runic readings are in no way a traditional fortune-telling tool. Instead, runes connect your intuition with your magic and the magic of the fates. When you can connect the past, present, and future through runic readings, you can change the outcome of your present and of your future. Think of it as divine intervention; if you knew the exact time and date of the next rainfall, would you hang your laundry out to dry? The answer is possibly yes, but you would bring it in before the rain began to fall. While the exact future is impossible to know because it is ever-changing, knowing some of the possible outcomes based on decisions you have made or will make allows you to be empowered in your life. Imagine having a business idea that could make millions, but you are unsure whether it would work. Asking your runes could give you the answer to the questions that are causing you uncertainty.

Those answers could have you being the CEO of your own successful business!

Don't be discouraged if, at first, you feel like the messages being received are not clear. It could be that you need to practice a little bit more or that you still need to trust your intuition completely. They don't call it 'practicing magic' for no good reason. In the beginning, you may want to practice single rune readings while you become accustomed to your runes—the way they feel and the energy they give off. Once you are more in tune, you can graduate to three rune casting, which we cover in a later chapter. This may seem like a lot to remember, but casting and reading your runes will become easier. Trust your instincts and your ability to tap into your magic to read your runes. If you feel that you are ready to perform a full casting, the chances are that you are ready, indeed. Your runes will communicate with you that they are prepared to give you the entire fate's message.

Translating Your Runic Information and Applying it to Your Life

You will need to remember that rune casting is in no way fortune-telling. Your runes will give you the answers you need to specific questions you ask. These questions may be anything from small insignificant decisions to life-altering decisions. Your runes are not cast at random and are explicitly placed for you by the fates, connecting your inner magic to theirs. In the same way, you used your intuition when asking for answers to your questions. You should take this same intuition out into the world as you make decisions that will alter your future. Looking out for opportunities and mindfully seeking the message the runes have given you will clearly see all potential outcomes.

For some, taking time out of their busy day to reflect on the day's happenings allows them to remember clearly how their runic reading relates to what has happened in a particular moment. This helps you be more in touch with your runes and the messages they are giving you and allows your intuition to develop and your magic to increase strength. Bear in mind that rune reading and casting is a form of magic. When you reject a moment or notion that you are being communicated with, you reject the magic as well. While this may seem trivial, rune readings are your magic, intimately interwoven with the magic of the universe or the fates. Because of that, you are not only rejecting the magic but rejecting yourself too. You are questioning your intuition and skewing the perspectives being given to you. Being stuck in a problem-solving mindset is part and parcel of being an adult. Your runes, however, are there to provide you with specific answers to these problems, and you will need to learn to trust your runes. This is a spiritual journey, one that requires you to be aware of the solution rather than trying to solve your way through the remainder of your life, ignoring their guidance.

The ancient Norse believed that the spoken word was more powerful than any other form of magic. In fact, they felt so strongly in this principle that they would speak their thoughts into existence. If this is not a testament to how strong their magic, and indeed your magic is, then we don't know what is. Write down all of your magic moments and show gratitude for being put onto the path you sought out. Believe wholeheartedly in yourself and your ability to change your future, and be confident of that ability. After all, you cannot expect others to see the magic in you if you are not prepared to embrace it fully within yourself. It is this belief that allows you to speak your possibilities into reality. Your runes may send your messages while you sleep. We cannot stress this enough. Pay attention to all messages and opportunities that come your way! Magic can be seen and found in the smallest of things around you, and when you are open to this, you are open to the messages the fates give you.

And finally, rune reading is a deeply spiritual form of magic that requires you to respect it in the same way it respects you. When you apply the changes or suggestions given to you during a reading, it is important to do so with the best intentions. To know with certainty that you are doing no harm is the only way to apply your runic readings to your life.

FIVE

Magic with Runes
────────────────

As we have discussed in previous chapters, runic wasn't just a writing system. Throughout history, it was used for magical purposes as well. This is particularly evident on swords and weapons where the inscriptions referred to the god Tyr. On Icelandic magical staves, curses and power inscriptions were often written. On Germanic coins, runic magic was evident to bring more money to the coin's spender or owner.

The people who used the runes for magic would cut branches from nut-bearing trees, carve the inscriptions on the wood, and cast these runes onto a white cloth. Prayers were offered up to the gods, while three runes were picked up randomly. These were then read if the gods permitted it. If not, a separate reading was done on another day.

While all runes were considered magical, the Ansuz and Tiwaz runes had significant magical powers in the Elder Futhark time. Some of these runes and inscriptions seemed meaningless but were later interpreted as chants for magical purposes. For charming purposes, the word Alu was used, and numerous artifacts have been found with this word carved on them. The meaning of Alu is still not specific. It appears that it represents a magical amulet, or at the very least is a metaphor for a magical amulet.

Similarly, in the Viking Ages, rings have been found with inscriptions. One of the most famous of these is the Kingmoor Ring, which is inscribed with the phrase 'runes of power.' The Björketorp and Stentoften stones were both inscribed with curses.

During the medieval ages, the Sigrdrifumal referred to runic magic. In a part of the poem, Sigrdrifa gives Sigurd an ale, charmed with the gladness rune. The poem mentions the charms of healing and spells of good fortune. In seven further stanzas, Sigrdrifa refers to magic runes and not divination with runes. Specifically, Tyr, Naudiz, and Laukaz are mentioned as being bewitched.

Other poems and chants of significance include the Hávamál, in which the divination refers to necromancy and healing. Throughout the ages, various clergy, authors, and tales have told of casting lots and casting magic with runes being carved or painted in everything from wood and stone to animal hide and blood. For example, the Armen runes have been cited as a place of magic and mysticism by authors Friedrich Bernhard Marby and Siegfried Adolph Kemmer and Karl Spiesberger, Stephen Flowers, Larry E. Camp, and Adolf Schleipfer. Although the proof is not irrefutable, with so much evidence and so many in the know coming forward to write about the magic and casting lots of runes, it's challenging to refute the esoteric claims.

Ralph Blum developed a set of runes used as 'lots' or fortune-telling systems in more modern times. Carved into clay, crystal, stones, or resin, these stones are chosen one at a time from a bag for readings. Later, authors Diana L. Paxson and Freya Aswynn wrote about the connection between runic divination and tarot reading.

A Written Language

Runologists may argue about the exact historical details of runic writings and their timeline. Still, there is a general guideline as to when runic began to emerge as a written text. It is presumed that the runic alphabet was derived from the old Latin alphabets as a secret text to keep historical and battle strategies from opposing armies during the battle for land. Later, it was discovered that these texts were sacred and had magical influence. Some historians say that runic dates back to 700 AD. In contrast, others believe that the text is much older and is far too formed and coherent for it to be dated to this specific time.

The oldest runic script has been dated back to the Meldorf brooch, before Christ. Perhaps the most famous early runic script appears on the Vimose Comb found in Denmark and dates back to 160 BC. It is this form of the Futhark, which is known to be an evolving script and language, that most scholarly articles credit as the Elder Futhark's first uniformed alphabetic appearance in the 1st century. While scholars will insist that the Futhark is, and was, an intentionally formed language for military purposes, studies show otherwise. The rune's association with the god Odin and its original meaning of a 'secret' seem to support the hypothesis that runic was meant to be a text learned by those seeking to enhance magic for manifestation purposes.

Perhaps the most fascinating aspect of the runic alphabet, besides its origins being shrouded in history, is the early variations. This suggests that the Futhark was never intended for one language and was instead meant to be a common thread between all Germanic people and tribes. The shapes, order, usage, and layout of runic writings have been different from the outset. So vast is this variation that the script may differ from family to family within the same region. Because of this, there is no such thing as a standardized runic alphabet. But instead, a social thread that connects the language and its people. This variation is especially apparent at around 700 CE when the Elder Futhark morphed into the Younger Futhark throughout the Scandinavian region and later when the Medieval Futhorc and Anglo-Saxon Futhorc reached the shores of Frisia and England.

When the runic alphabet reached Ireland and some Scotland areas, specifically Orkney, it began to be used by the local people. The Vikings who had invaded Britain and its surrounding regions sought to intermingle with the common folk. Some think this was a strategic move to win the local people's favor while moving for the throne. Others believe that it was the magic of the Celts that drew the Vikings to them. Druids (Celtic pagan priests) began consulting with the Vikings on matters about magic. This consultation led to a beautiful and powerful unity of two magics and scripts. This was the birth of powerful new magic that encompassed Celtic symbolism and runic writings. So respected was this new magic that clergy, chieftains, and counselors of the Anglo-Saxon royalty, despite being Christian, would gather to strategize in meetings they called 'Ruens.'

In fact, in the 4th century, when Bishop Wulfila translated the Christian bible into Gothic, he named it the 'Runa,' which translates to 'mystery.' This combination of scripts, cultures, histories, and magic could be seen as nothing more than ease of communication when remembering that runic was a written and spoken language that transcended conventional territorial language. We choose to believe that combining two cultures whose spirituality was deeply rooted in magic, the gods, and the fates.

Traditional Celtic card or stone readings began to give way to rune usage. It wasn't long before the power of this written language became apparent. Runes and runic inscriptions throughout this area show a beautiful symbiosis of runic and Gaelic symbolism and new lores, which included Odin, spread throughout Ireland and Scotland. Some would argue that England and its territories were never stronger than when it was under Viking rule when the scripts and magic amalgamated. As the Viking king Cnut ascended to the throne as the King of all England, runic halted the more popular Latin scripts' spread. Instead, it appeared as if written languages took a step backward in history. The truth was that although the rest of Europe saw the Vikings as heathens and savages, the reintroduction of runic was strategic.

Through the spread of Christianity, Latin was now widely used by most of Europe, including France, seeking to take land from the British. The introduction of runic to the people of Britain and its territories allowed for battle strategies to be thought out and passed on in secret and ensured that it would not be decrypted by other nations who were not privy to runic. This political, military and esoteric strategy had the Vikings seated on England's throne for the better part of a century.

The throne was never regained by the Anglo-Saxons by force. This was impossible with the runic and Celtic belief systems in place. Instead, the House of Wessex regained the throne through a treaty that allowed the Vikings to continue to inhabit and use the lands of Ireland, Scotland, and the British ports. Celtic and Gaelic traditional writings, therefore, continued to be heavily influenced by the runic alphabet. While not many runic writings remain in these areas today, those who have been found and are movable have been returned to Scandinavia's people to preserve their ancient script's history. Those who are immovable or which show strong Celtic or Gaelic writings remain as a stark reminder of the power of the Vikings and their runic magic. The influence of runic in Britain and its territories is often overlooked as a brief moment in time when a foreign people occupied and ruled these lands. However, runic writing and the magic it embodied had a prolific and lasting impression on Britain's people. Many modern divination tools from this area continue to incorporate runic script. Most will tell you that they are entirely unaware that the two symbolisms were once separate.

The Magic Within

For years people believed that magic was exclusively a set of beliefs or rituals to manipulate natural and supernatural forces. Totally independent of religion, tribes, and cultures have been involved in magic since the dawn of time. Categorized as witches or wizards by the Christian faith, the truth is that magic has been used for medicinal purposes, even in the upsurge of Christianity. To this day, some people practice magic to improve their lives, connect with fate, as herbal medicine and tinctures, and get answers to their unasked questions.

In the past, people believed that some were born with more power than others. The truth is that everyone has magic within them, and all people can harness that power. Since the nineteenth century, and despite the persecution of pagans and so-called witches, people have used magic. In fact, at times during the 1800s, science was considered magical. It became the norm for anything outside of Western Christianity to be considered magic, but not all magic was deemed equal. It was this belief that had the church categorize magic. While magic is meant to be selfless and assist people, some types, such as curses, were classified as black magic. White magic was considered magic, which helped in the healing of someone, or magic, which was beneficial to others. Neutral magic or gray magic was performed for no specific gain, and this is where runic magic seemed to fit in.

To others, at least in the beginning, runes were arbitrary incantations or references to random physical bodies. It was only later that tribes and cultures outside of the Germanic people realized the purpose of the runic alphabet and how deeply it connected those who practiced to the fates and gods. And this brings us to the magic within every person. Magic may be categorized into black, grey, and white. Still, it is the practitioners of this magic who can nurture the magic they have been bestowed. Those who practice magic and are deeply in touch with this aspect have studied and immersed themselves in their magic. In times gone by, practicing low magic would be considered a lesser offense and would perhaps not have been punished with death. But, the fact remains that likely everyone practices low magic every day. Simple rituals such as meditation, prayer, or conversations with oneself all fall within the spectrum of low magic. Manifestation and positive affirmations are both magics that are being offered out to the universe in an attempt to change or better one's life.

In the early 90s, Stephan Grundy said that runic magic was the active participation in magic. This means that when the runes are used for their intended purposes, the magic happens through manifestation or through the reader's answers when asking a question of the fates. Unlike Shaman magic, runic magic seeks to enhance the magic within a person rather than relying on outside entities to invoke magic. Grundy reemphasized that each rune had a sound and a deeper meaning, which was meant to connect the owner of the message to the rune.

SIX

Getting Acquainted With Your Runes

When deciding which runes to buy or make for yourself, the first question asked is usually, "Which rune set is the right one for me?" As we will mention later, choosing your runes is a deeply personal journey. You may want to ask yourself whether you intend on having more than one set if you see yourself making your own runes. If using runes will be a hobby or something that will be with you actively for the rest of your life.

If you are buying your runes premade, they will probably be the Elder Futhark version. This is simply because there is more information readily available on this version. This is not to say that you have to stick to the Elder version of the runes. More complex questions may require the Younger Futhark to provide more precise answers. The positioning of your runes will mean different things, and these will be explained in a dedicated section of this book. It is important to note that if you plan on reading reverse and converse runes, the Elder Futhark is a better option for divination purposes.

Once you begin to shop around for your runes, you should first be in the right mental space. Do you like the way the prospective runes look and feel? Do the runes draw you to them? When you hold the runes, do they speak to you and make you feel a strong connection with them?

Historically speaking, runes aren't really passed down unless they are given from and to someone who knows the history and the intention behind the magic used with those particular runes. If you choose a secondhand rune set, make sure that you know its history well and pay special attention to your intuition and how the runes make you feel. Some runes are explicitly used for magical purposes and cannot be used for divination. In this case, you may want to get a magic set and a divination set. Lastly, the more you use your runes, the more you will connect with them. Your runes will connect with you, gaining and feeding off of your inner magic and your personality.

Choosing Your Runes

Choosing your runes is a deeply personal decision that depends on your purpose for owning the runes and your own set of moral principles. You will need to consider the material and whether you are vegan and against, say, antler as a material. You should consider your own aesthetic as well as what material you feel most connected to. Mastering the runic alphabet, runic divination, and magic may take years, but being connected to your runes will help to develop the magic inside of you.

Scholars, to this day, debate the reason and origin of the runic alphabet. Still, there is a general consensus that the Elder Futhark, and later, its spin-offs were used for magical and divination purposes. The Elder Futhark, the most well known and most used Runic system, has 24 symbols. For the most part, people will choose the Elder Futhark purely based on the abundance of information available on it. This is not to say that choosing a newer version is wrong. Still, information on these younger versions is limited. It could become frustrating as the script became outlawed with the rise of Christianity.

Every rune serves three purposes; its sound (phoneme), which begins with the letter of the alphabet, a physical object, which may seem vague or completely mundane, and its esoteric or mystical meaning. When casting your and reading your runes, you must be in touch with your inner intuition; the purpose of a runic reading is to receive information from the past, present, and future. Without this intuition, the powerful meaning of your runes may be lost. Remember that a single runic symbol is meant to speak volumes to you.

Now that you have a basic idea of what your runes can do for you and the history behind runic, it is essential to decide on your material choice. Which runic alphabet you will use, and whether you will make your own runes or purchase an already made set. Making your own runes can be a profoundly intimate process. Through mindfulness and meditation, you will be able to infuse your own energy into your runes as you carve or paint them into your chosen material. The material you choose will depend much on your skill level and your ability to get your hands on the right tools. Etching or carving runes into stone or wood would be far more complicated than, say, painting them onto something. Having said that, making your own runes is an amazing outlet to express your creativity and become one with your runes.

To make your own Elder Futhark runes, you will need to choose what material your runes will be placed onto. Each rune will need to be around the same size. Remember that if you are going to source your runes from nature, you should always practice good magical etiquette to infuse your runes with the goodness from their onset. It is important to remember that some carving materials will be more challenging than others. For example, the rock will be more durable than clay, and untreated clay that isn't cured will begin to chip and crack if not clear-varnished. It is essential to keep in mind the purpose of your runes and whether they will be traveling around with you. Those that will be moved around in a pouch, for example, will need to be more durable than those stored at home in a wooden box.

Should you choose to purchase your runes, you will find a massive variety on the market. Runes are available in all kinds of materials and can be carved, etched, or painted. Sets will usually consist of 24 Elder Futhark runes with a blank tile representing the Wyrd rune. Storing your runes is equally as important, but this will be addressed further along in the chapter. Store-bought runes may come with a set of instructions as well as a breakdown of the meaning of each rune. This makes it easier for beginners to delve into the world of runic magic. Keep in mind that the art of reading runes varies hugely, and you will need to trust your gut in finding a method that works well for you.

As mentioned before, the material on which your rune is carved needs to make a magical personal connection with you. Still, the budget may also play a role. Some of the materials available are as follows:

Bone Runes

Made from the cleaned bones of animals, bone runes are usually hand-painted or engraved with the runic symbol. Find yourself gravitating towards a bone collection or have a bone collection. This may be the right material for you. Historically, bone runes were used by witches who had a magical connection to animals. It is believed that the animal's spirit remains in the bone and assists the possessor with their magic.

Antler Runes

These are made from deer antlers and possess similar magical properties to bone runes. If you are a person who has a deep connection to Stag energy or find yourself drawn to these creatures, antler runes would be an excellent choice to connect your inner magic with the rune.

Wooden Runes

For magical purposes, oak, ash, and elder wood are preferred, but other wood varieties are also used. What is important with wooden runes is the personal connection one has to the tree. Most wood runes are painted or wood-burned and sealed with a clear varnish to protect them. If you choose to leave your runes untreated, it is best to rub them down every now and again with a light oil or beeswax to keep them from chipping or cracking.

Stone Runes

Stone runes cover a wide variety of materials. Made from precious gems, semi-precious stones, and pebbles, stone runes have become more prevalent in the modern ages. The ancient Nordic people believed that runes needed to be carved into wood, bone, or antler for the real magic to come through. Having said that, gemstones, crystals, and indeed rock and stone have proved to be of massive magical significance throughout the ages. Used mostly by Wiccans, stone runes are beautiful to work with and are incredibly aesthetically pleasing. When choosing your stone rune, one can draw on the stone's inherent power. When choosing pebbles, one can choose from an area that is particularly emotionally or magically significant.

Ceramic Tile Runes

These runes are most popular with people who choose to make their own runes. The act of creating, kiln-firing, and carving your own rune is incredibly intimate, and you can pour your own energy and intentions into the rune. Make sure to adequately seal your runes to ensure that they are durable, though.

Glass Runes

Probably the most difficult runes, glass runes are exclusively made by people. While they are absolutely acceptable in the practice of runic magic, it is important to consider the intent behind the creation of the rune before purchasing it from a third party.

Now that you have decided what material you will use for your runes, the size and shape come into play. While the material is important for magical purposes, the size is more about practicality. Create a too small rune, and you may not be able to read it. Too large, and it will be cumbersome to cast. The size should be relatively uniform to prevent inadvertently influencing how you would pull the stones from their pouch or box through the familiarity of size. Remember that some readers choose to read their runes in reverse and have a different meaning when they land face-down or upside-down. Runes that are too rounded may be difficult to read if they are reversed. Once again, it is important to choose something that works for you, connecting you to the magic within.

How to Use Your Runes

For centuries, runes have been used as an oracle for anyone seeking to know the answers to questions that are plaguing them. With a history that dates back to the ancient Germanic and Nordic tribes, runes are still used today by modern Oracles and users of magic. While some may want to receive a reading from those who have mastered runes, others choose to learn to read runes themselves. With a meaning as mysterious as runic magic and the runic alphabet itself, runes are often made of materials that have a connection or meaning to the runes owner. Today, the more popular Elder Futhark is used for oracle, magical, and divination purposes. Still, other forms of the ancient alphabet can be used. We have provided a section in Chapter 2 on each specific rune's meanings for those who choose to use the Younger Futhark or Anglo-Saxon Futhorc. It is important to remember that runes have a threefold meaning. The reading of runes is mainly reliant on one's inner intuition.

Most will agree that runes were used as an alphabetic system by the Germanic and Nordic tribes. What is still debatable is how deeply rooted runic writings are in magic and oracle divination. What is known is that most runic inscriptions seem to have had at least some form of chant, incantation, curse, or desired result in them. This is probably most obvious with runic inscriptions found on weapons and warnings to not desecrate burial grounds and sacrificial areas.

In ancient times, and now, runic magic and divination can be a potent tool to assist you through problematic areas of your life or guidance through specific issues you may be facing. Runes are not a fortune-telling tool but instead allow you advice on how to react or behave if events do occur in your lie. While this form of non-clarity may seem frustrating, runic magic relies heavily on your intuition. on your ability to focus on asking questions that are specific to issues about you.

Masters of runic magic will tell you from the offset that the future is not fixed and that one's fate is continually changing. By default, if you know what your future is, you can change the outcome. A runic reading outcome can be changed based solely on the fact that a person now intuitively knows the answer to the question they asked. Because of this, runes can help a person make decisions, change situations, or make decisions based on the rune readings.

We need to reiterate that rune casting is not fortune-telling! The runes will only give you the answers to specific questions or issues plaguing your conscious or unconscious mind. Runes that are cast are not random. They are a placement by the fates through your own inner magic to help you clarify the issues in your life and reconnect you with the universe and the fates. If there is an issue that is worrying you, you could try focusing on that issue or ask the question aloud. It is important that your mind is clear and focused on your runes as they are cast. When you cast your runes in this way, you are most likely to get the most precise answers to your question and will be able to see the potential outcomes clearly.

Another important factor when casting your own runes or

casting runes for others is the material on which the runes are inscribed or painted. We have covered each type of material quite extensively. Still, We need to reiterate that magical connection you have with your runes. Specific runes readers seem to have more power than others. This is almost certainly because the runes owner has a strong emotional and magical connection with the type of rune and may have been practicing runic magic for some time.

When setting up a runic reading, a piece of cloth or fabric, known as a rune cloth, should be placed in the reading area. Most times, this cloth is white and is designed explicitly for runic readings. It is entirely up to you to decide what size, fabric, and pattern speak to you, magically. Other than the practicality of the cloth protecting your runes when casting, it acts as a spiritual and magical boundary during the cast.

Like every other kind of magic, it will take time to master reading your runes. While books and guides can help you understand what each of your runes are trying to communicate to you, it will be up to you to interpret those meanings and apply them to your life. In the meantime, this book will provide you with a go-to guide with easy reference to the actual symbols, their meanings, and their esoteric or runic meanings.

It is perfectly normal to feel unsure at first. Still, as you begin to trust your intuition more, you will be able to understand the message being portrayed to you with greater ease. If you are still unsure, you can always write down the runes or the runes' order and refer back to them as time goes on and the fates play out. In this way, you can better connect with the fates and understand the next time a message similar to that comes up during a casting. Remember that when a rune presents itself upside down during your casting, there will be an alternative message. Rune casting is not a perfect science. Even the masters of runic reading will admit that the significance of reading may not become apparent until later. If you have chosen a set of runes containing a blank rune, it is meant as a representation of the rune Wyrd and represents all runes. This is an especially important rune as it urges the reader to look deeply within. It is a reminder that everything that has happened to you up to this moment are actions you have put into place. Some runic readers choose not to include the blank or Wyrd rune in their readings. This is purely a personal preference.

Respecting the Magic in You

As we mentioned before, everyone has magic within them. In the days gone by, this realization was far more prevalent than today, with magic, Wicca, and the like being largely tabooed with Christianity's rise. Those who become in tune with the magic within have often said that they feel a deeper connection to the world, nature, and themselves. There is something incredibly mysterious about people who have uncovered their own magic. As children, we are often drawn to these people. Placing them on a pedestal, believing them to have 'superpowers.' The truth is, those people believed wholeheartedly in their own power and have practiced over the years to understand what that magic meant to them.

If you are reading this book, chances are that there is a spark of realization that you too have that magic inside you. You are yearning to unlock that potential or find answers to your spiritual journey. For most, the issue is that religion indoctrinates that magic is bad when, in fact, there is no reason why the two cannot coexist. In Christianity, people believe in miracles, a simple act that dictates that a higher power creates an unexpected result. This is no different from a person manifesting their desires or asking the fates for a different path. Magic in itself is defined as "an extraordinary power or influence seemingly from a supernatural source." This definition, in itself, insinuates that changing one's life path is powerful and magical. By consciously creating your life and experience, you are, in fact, tapping into the magic which is inside of you. The tricky part is that you are human, emotional, flexible, and easily distracted.

Most of us are not prepared to accept that our life's most painful experiences are often brought on by our own decisions. We are even more reluctant to accept that these experiences offer us the most profound lessons. When you can accept that your fate is not cast in stone and that you do indeed possess magic inside you, you can change your life's outcome. More importantly, though, you will need to take responsibility for your newfound power and be prepared to nurture it as you learn to grow into your new self. Magic relies heavily on a person's intuition and on their ability to consciously harness that magic. This can be done by learning to respect yourself and your magic in various ways. In the past, those who practiced magic lived by a specific set of principles, covered below.

Inward Reflection

When you take time out of your busy daily schedule to reflect on what is happening in your subconscious and to empty your mind of negativity and ill-thoughts, you are better able to harness your magic for divination purposes. The very act of clearing one's mind may seem easy, but it's a lot harder than you think. With outside distractions and the stress of modern-day living, it is absolutely vital to take some time every single day to practice the art of inward reflection to connect with yourself spiritually.

Intent

A little further in this chapter, we will discuss the Rule of Three, but the intent is massive in the realms of magic. When casting, chanting, or performing divinations, your objective should be pure. Intent goes hand in hand with inward reflection as you cannot cast with malicious intent. People, anger, and ego drive our actions far too often, and magic has a way of ensuring that balance is restored when the intent is not pure.

Gratitude

You're magical, wonderful, and powerful! This is something that should be savored and respected. When your runes are cast, and the meanings become clear, it is important to show up thanks for the messages and directions you give. It is easy to forget that although magic is given to everyone, it is not a given.

Being Mindful of Your Emotions

We have spoken about intent, but your emotions can often cloud your intentions and your intuition. By keeping your emotions in check or only performing your divinations and castings when your feelings are not in absolute turmoil, you can better read and accept the messages given to you. While this may seem counterintuitive, it is important to not cast when you are outraged or nursing a bruised ego.

The Rule of Three

Revered as the most important rule of all magic, this is of absolute importance. The Rule of Three dictates that whatever you put out into the word will be returned to you threefold. Remember how we spoke of intent? This is where casting with pure intentions becomes incredibly important as the balance of magic always needs to be restored.

Known by many names, karma, for instance, the Rule of

Three reminds a person to always remember that life is a series of causes and effects. Runic readings in themselves are centered around the principle of three; past, present, and future. Readings offer guidance on lessons that have been learned or should be learned to change one's life for the better.

Magic is a balancing act of action, reward, or consequence, much like life is. Until recently, it was believed that the rule of three was incorporated into magic by the Christian uprising. Still, similar texts and Rule of Three writings have been found predating the Christian faith. Whether you choose to believe in the Rule of Three, it is a stark reminder that cause and effect are ever-present in our lives. Acting with ill intent or out of anger will result in the magical balance being restored in favor of the person who endured the ill intent.

SEVEN

Casting and Reading

KNOWING THE HISTORY AND THE SIGNIFICANT MEANINGS OF your runes is essential when beginning your journey into divination with them. As we have ascertained, runic appeared to have been a written and spoken language, but, historically, its primary purpose was for divination magic. We have learned from the ancient texts, and the information gathered over years of study that runes rely on intuition. The Vikings believed this intuition was the thread that bound us as people to the gods and fate. When you learn to read your runes and open your mind to the possibilities they present to you, you develop your intuition and strengthen your magic. Understanding that magic is something that you have always possessed. Learning to nurture your intuition while following the advice of those who came before you will unlock your hidden divination powers. It will bring together your past, present, and future.

But let's begin with what 'casting' is. Diviners use various forms to cast their runes to read what message the fates are sending. To cast your runes means randomly selecting runes from their pouch or box and placing them in a specific pattern, some of which are mentioned below. Alternately, you can gently throw them onto your ceremonial rune cloth, altar, or reading board. Think about casting a fishing line. You know there are fish, either intuitively or because you asked yourself a series of questions to determine your fishing spot. Then, you cast your line and wait for the fish to bite. Casting runes is no different. You've asked the question, and once you cast your runes, you will receive the answers you requested.

Oracular Divination

Oracles were people who were revered for being able to provide wise counsel as well as predicting the future. Most oracles would call on a deity to give this information. Still, external magical tools such as runes were often used. Derived from the Latin word for 'speak,' Oracles often used divination to tell the fortune of those who sought answers to pressing issues in their lives. This form of divination was thought to be a portal between mortals and the fates and was considered some of the highest forms of magic.

In Norse mythology, Odin sacrificed himself to gain the knowledge of the runes and used the head of the god Mimir as a form of oracular divination. Today, the magic of the runes and our own intuitive magic still provide valuable insight. Insight into the past, present, and future, binding us to the fates and allowing us to make decisions that could alter our lives.

Your Runic Pattern and Readings

In a typical casting, a lot is left to chance, and it is for this reason, you will need to have full trust in your intuition and your runes. When you randomly throw your runes onto your rune cloth, you are essentially giving that moment to the fates and telling them that you trust their answers entirely.

Traditional rune castings usually relate to the past,

present, and future, and the runes that land face up are the runes that will be read. Runes that are reversed or land outside of their normal position do not always mean something negative. On the contrary, it usually means that the caster and reader need to pay exceptional care and attention to that specific rune. A rune that lands sideways depicts a flipped or opposite meaning. As an example, your rune landing upright and in the correct position usually means turmoil or tribulation. Your sideways rune would mean the exact opposite and would depict peace or calm. A conversed rune (a rune that lands with its symbol facing downward) or rune that lands upright in its usual position has the normal meaning. A reversed rune (a rune that reads right to left) would have the opposite meaning in the downward position. Converse runes usually mean that the reason for the rune appearing is a secret. The answer may not be apparent or will only become obvious further into the future. When runes appear in this way, it is a good idea to write them in your rune diary. This way, you can come back to that particular casting to analyze and meditate on it. Finally, look out for the Wyrd rune, which is a strong suggestion that you are not and cannot be in control of your situation as the fates are guiding your life entirely right now.

Once you are ready to cast your stones and begin your reading, find a quiet area. Take a deep breath, clear your mind of all distractions, and focus on what question you will ask. Think clearly and precisely, and ensure that your question stays at the forefront of your conscious thought. Some readers chat, pray, hum, or call on a deity for guidance through their reading. Again, this is entirely preferential.

With your rune cloth in front of you, you are now ready to begin your casting. It may be easier for beginners to pick a rune from its bag or box, then analyze it and think about its significance before placing it on the rune cloth. If you are content that you know what the rune is telling you and how it pertains to your question, you can continue by selecting another rune.

Like all other types of oracle readings, there are various forms of runic readings. The most common of these are discussed below.

Three Rune Layouts

Perfect for beginner readers, the three rune layout allows the caster to randomly select three runes from their storage container and place them on the rune cloth. The runes should be placed as follows:

Rune one on the right, rune two in the middle, and rune three on the left.

This means your runes are ordered three, two, one when read from left to right.

Rune one is a representation of what question, situation, or conscious issue you are questioning.

Rune two is the challenge you are facing.

Rune three is the action required to change or better the situation you have queried of the fates.

Triple Runes

2

Present Influences

1

Upcoming Challenges
What You Need To Do

3

Outcome

YOU

Three Norns

Past Actions — What Will Likely Happen — What Is Influencing You Now

YOU

Spiritual Three Rune Cast

Your Physical Condition — Your Mental Condition — Your Spiritual Condition

YOU

Five Rune Layouts

A five rune cast is similar to the three rune cast in that five runes are selected at random from their container and placed on your rune cloth. However, the placement of these runes is different.

Rune one must be placed in the middle of the rune cloth. All other runes selected will form a cross on your rune cloth.

Rune two should be placed to the left of your center rune in the west position.

Rune three will be placed on top of the center rune in the north position.

Rune four should be placed below the center rune in the south position.

Finally, rune five should be placed to the right of the center rune in the east position.

The runes can be placed face down and turned as you read them, or you can choose to place them face up if they will not distract you. Be careful not to disturb the rune's position; runes upside down or inverted will have a different meaning. Runes in this pattern should be read in rune two, rune one, and rune five. This represents the past, present, and future of your life. Rune four in the south position represents the issue or question at hand and which elements of that issue should be accepted. Rune three, in the east position, is the solution or the guidance required for your question.

Five Rune Cast

Nine Rune Cast

Norse mythology places emphasis on the number nine as an incredibly magical number. Historically, the nine rune cast was used to determine where a person was on their spiritual journey and what potential changes and opportunities were written in the fates. This type of cast requires a deep intuition and connection to your runes as you will need to be very in touch with what you lack in spirituality. To do a nine-run casting, you will need to randomly pick nine runes out of their container. Each rune should be held and contemplated on for a little while before scattering it randomly on your rune cloth.

The nine rune cast is not an accurate reading. Still, as has been practiced for centuries, the rune which lands closest to the center of your rune cloth relates to your current situation. Those lying closest to the edges are less important to the reading. If your rune is close to or touching another rune, it means that these two factors influence each other. Runes on opposite sides of the rune cloth are opposing solutions or influences. Runes that land face up are of particular importance in this type of casting. Those that have landed face down are of lesser immediate significance. Make sure to keep those that have landed face down in their original position. These are the runes that are representative of outside influences in your life or future potential possibilities. This is where your intuition comes in handy. Because the future is entirely malleable and changeable, according to your actions, your runes will be heavily reliant on your interpretation and own magic in giving you the answers to your future.

Nine Grid Cast

Hidden Future Influences That Will Keep Away Positive | Best Possible Outcome | Your Feelings About Outcome

Present Hidden Influences | Present Influences | Your Present Feelings

Past Hidden Influences | Past Influences | Your Past Feelings

YOU

EIGHT

Storing Your Runes

There is no specific good or bad way to store your runes. For some, the vessel that holds their runes is as important as choosing their runes. For practical purposes, a soft pouch is best to travel with your runes. This will make sure that your runes don't get damaged in transit or while not in use. Some prefer to store their runes in a wooden box on display. If you choose to use a wooden box to keep your runes, it may be best to look for boxes made out of wood considered sacred. Boxes made out of alder wood, applewood, ash, and elder are quite freely available, and all come with magical significance. You may want to line the inside of your box with a clean cloth to ensure that your runes don't rub together. Generally speaking, there is no correct vessel to store your runes in. Their storage is mostly for practical purposes, but choosing the right type of material can help keep your runes magical charged when not in use.

The Magical Significance of Wood Boxes

Choosing to store your runes in a wooden box may have a double use. The box does not only protect your runes from getting damaged, but the wood itself can help to keep your runes charged with the type of energy you choose. While cloth bags don't make much of a difference to your runes' energy, the right type of wood may give your runes that extra edge you are looking for.

Alderwood – As masculine energy, the alder tree was known to be sacred by the Celts. Alderwood holds the properties of confidence, bravery, and spiritual growth and shielding one from spiritual attack.

Applewood – The apple tree is synonymous with feminine energy and fertility. Applewood holds the properties of purity and light and gives the ability to receive visions.

Ash – Ash is associated with female energy and more effeminate male energy. The ash tree is sacred to the Celts, and it is sacred to Odin in Norse mythology. Wood from an ash tree holds artistic magic and was used to keep sea monsters at bay when the Vikings were voyaging at sea.

Beechwood – Associated with masculine energy, beechwood, and oak are very closely related. Nordic pagans considered the beech tree to be sacred and associated it with old wisdom, desire, and victory.

Birchwood – The birch tree is considered sacred and represents new beginnings, spiritual cleansing, and rebirth. Associated with female energy, birchwood is strongly related to maternal intuition.

Cedar – King Solomon, who is known to be one of the greatest mystics ever, created his temple and chariot out of cedar. It is associated with protection, preservation, and conjuring spirits as well as invocations.

Elder – While some may associate wood from elder trees with bad luck, the truth is that it protects against and promotes imagination and change. The bad luck rumor started when the elder was used for crucifixions, specifically Christ's crucifixion.

Elm – As a feminine energy wood, wood from elm trees is

known for stave off lightning strikes. Elm represents rebirth, fertility, harvest, and spirituality in the magic realm.

Oak – Oak is a masculine energy tree and is considered to be sacred. Oak is said to amplify magic and, as such, was highly sought after in the magical world. Oak is associated with healing, intuition, and observation.

Vine – Representing masculine and feminine energies, wood from vine trees is associated with spiritual contact, connecting with sacred knowledge and rebirth.

Willow – Connected with feminine energy, the willow tree is highly sacred. Associated with water and the spirit or soul, wood from willows aligns itself to its owner's energy. An excellent storage option for divination tools, willow has been known to strengthen one's third eye and intuition.

NINE

Consecrating Your Runes

Before and after using your runes, it is a good idea to consecrate them. This will ensure that you are cleansing your runes of any bad energy that may have been imparted on them and will keep them charged for readings to be more precise and accurate. To consecrate something means to make it holy, and it is this process that will reconnect you to your runes and your runes to the fates and the gods. As we have already discussed, your runes can help you open your intuition and own magic and are there to help you get back on your life path.

Before you begin consecrating your runes, you must be in the right frame of mind so that you do not accidentally impart negative energy into your runes. You will need to feel a connection to your rune not only before a reading but before consecrating and cleansing your runes. Just as there are many different types of runes to choose from, there are various ways in which you can choose to consecrate your runes. Some readers don't believe in consecration at all. In contrast, others believe it is an integral ritual to keep your runes free of negativity and correctly charged. Below we will highlight some of the more popular forms of consecrating your runes. There is no right or wrong way to connect with and cleanse your runes. Remember that if you choose to consecrate your runes, connect to your runes, and invite positivity and enlightenment.

The Sage Method

Sage is a sacred plant in many cultures. It is believed that the smoke from burning sage purifies the physical and spiritual areas in a person's life. If the smell of fresh burning sage is too overpowering for you, you can always use incense. Should sage or sage incense not be available to you, another sacred incense can be used, such as frankincense or myrrh. For those who are intolerant of scents, use another method.

Begin by lighting your sage or incense and allowing the smoke to plume over you, your space, and the bag or box where you store your runes. Next, pick up each rune individually with your receptive hand; this is the hand you don't write with. Hold the rune for a moment in contemplation. Hold the rune over the smoke of the incense or sage before placing it on your rune cloth. You can ask your guides, angels, or deities to protect you or bless you with high magic. You can also choose to look at the runes laid out on your rune cloth and contemplate on the meaning of each one, connecting with its energy. Feel your mind, body, and spirit connecting with the rune and become a part of it. Some choose to say a prayer, chant, or meditation before ending their consecration. It is entirely up to you whether you decide to bless your runes so that they may help others as well as you.

The Candle Consecration

Most choose to use a pure white candle when using this method, but you may choose to use a candle with a color that speaks to your soul or has a deeper meaning to you. Begin by lighting your candle and allowing the warm glow to wash over you, calming your mind and body. Take a moment to meditate and focus on the consecration. Now place your runes to the left of the candle, being sure to keep your mind clear. When you are ready, pick up a rune being sure to pause to meditate on its meaning before you pass it through the candle flame. Make sure that you are careful and do not burn yourself. Once you are done with your meditation, put the rune on its cloth on the right side of the candle, repeating the process with your other runes. As with the sage method, it is entirely up to you whether you want to chant, pray, or meditate before you end your consecration.

Water Consecration

Water has long been used as a cleansing form, not only for the body but also for the mind and soul. To consecrate your runes with the water method, you will need a small bowl of water and a candle of your choice. Light the candle and place it to the left of your bowl. Place your rune bag to the left of the candle. Select a rune at random from its bag or box and drop a little water on it. See the water run over the rune, and with your receptive hand, trace the rune symbol with your finger, taking time to say its name and connect with it on a deeper level. Slowly pass your rune through the candle, taking care not to burn yourself before placing the rune on the right side of the candle on your rune cloth. At this point, you can choose to say the rune's name once more, chant, pray, or meditate for a moment before selecting another rune and beginning the process again.

Rune Chants

You may choose to make your own chant that can be said when consecrating your runes. If you are not quite ready to create your own chant or prayer, you are welcome to use one of these chants as a simple way to connect with your runes during the consecration.

Chant 1
Ancient symbol of wisdom and secret behold.
May the fates deem me worthy of the answers you hold.
My intuition guides me and my words.
Impart your wisdom so that you may be heard.
My heart and mind is open to your wisdom I will receive,
And I will be good and just with what has been conceived.

Chant 2
These, my runes of power,
These my runes of sight.
I ask of all who listen,
Will you grant me the sight?
I strive to be one with you,
And if you choose to show me the way,
Present your symbols
So that I may know the answers, I pray.

Chant 3
These, my symbols here on wood.
My symbols are drawn on stone and bone.
I ask the fates to intervene and ask that I cast my first stone.
These sacred symbols will reveal my fate,
They will show me the truths to be sewn.
My fate is yours,
The magic is ours, and the future is mine to be known.

Conclusion

People have always sought to communicate with each other, whether through signs, language, or written text. While this was purely a form of communication for some, it was a way to create their own destiny, tap into their own inner powers, and harness the earth's magic. Runic was thought to be a form of writing that was used by the ancient Germanic tribes. Used to restrict physical property or charms, spells, blessings, and curses, runic became a powerful divination tool to tell one's fortune.

Scholars dated the language back to at least the 1st century. Still, some believe that it had been used for at least 100 years prior because of its advanced formation. So ancient is the language that some scripts have been found in tombs that have dated back to Christ. While some of the details about the origins of runic may still be sketchy, what is certain is that it was widely used by the 1st century. Although the script peaked and eventually gave way to the more modern Latin alphabets, runic is still used today in some regions of Scandinavia.

As an alphabet and as a spoken and written language, runes have a complex and rich history. This history varies

Conclusion

depending on who you talk to. Scholars claim that it was used as a form of secret language to avoid detection by the invading Greek and Roman empires; others cite its origins in Norse mythology. It is these mythological claims that gave runes the reputation of being the embodiment of magic. The very word rune means secret or whisper. When it spread to the United Kingdom's shores, even Irish Gaelic took on the definition as a mystery.

The origins and meaning of the word rune should give away the power that runic held. The scripts' cultural significance, history, and the power they held for the Scandinavian and North Germanic people is epic and has survived time itself. The fact that the runic alphabet cannot be traced back to any definitive authoritarian figure driving its usage or that no scholar can definitively record its earliest usage should be a testament to how mysterious this language is. With plausible theories on how runic eventually made its way throughout the world, the script's origins have people wondering how a relatively unknown language came from nowhere and somehow managed to evolve and remain prevalent until the 17th century.

There are currently only a few runic script categories; these have been covered in this book. It is notable that outside of the Futhark and Futhorc scripts mentioned in previous chapters, other runic forms are still being discovered and deciphered. Currently, the Elder Futhark has the most information available, not only on its history but also on its esoteric use. This may be because it was the most commonly used runic script. Those who still use the runic script in Denmark continue to evolve and adapt the script to remain a secret. So absolute is the belief of these new runic cultures in the legend of Odin sacrificing himself. They believe that one needs to be worthy to gain the knowledge of modern-day runic. It's difficult not to speculate when stories of magic and castings are brought up, especially when a person understands how inti-

Conclusion

mately interwoven the script was with magic throughout the Viking Age. While it is true that some inscriptions have been found with nothing more than an ownership message, the fact remains that a great many runic finds have included at least an insinuation of magic.

Magical words of curses and healing, as well as tales of necromancy, have been translated and are both terrifying and fascinating. The parallel to modern religion has a person wondering how many of these fables were drawn from when modern religions' creation overtook paganism. A person can take away from all these stories because runes were powerful. The messages of magic carved into objects needed to be noticed. Runic writings, which warned against the desecration of burial, sacrificial and sacred lands began to be heeded, even by those who sought to spread Christianity. While the remainder of the world seemed to be converting to this new faith, Vikings held onto their belief systems. They had an almost supernatural relationship with their gods, and the omens they thought were sent to them. Something as trivial as a flock of birds flying in a specific formation was, to the Vikings, a message which was to be observed and used to guide them through events to come. It is believed that runic magic still exists today because of this omen reading and how the Viking people connected and remained connected to their magic. Runes and runic magic are still practiced in some parts of Denmark today, a testament to the tenacity of the runic script and the magical modern-day Vikings hold onto. The beauty of runic magic requires no particular skill and enhances a person's own intuition and inner magic. It is a guide, a means of reconnecting a person to their spirituality and gaining access to the intuitive knowledge they already possess but cannot otherwise access.

Your journey with runic magic will be a profoundly personal one. one in which you will learn to identify the language of the messages being sent to you and the connec-

Conclusion

tion of your magic to your runes' magic. The thread that intertwines your past, present, and future to the fates and the decisions you have made up until this point will become clear. This clarity will allow you to change your path and fulfill the destiny that was written for you. As you learn to grow into your magic, your respect for an infinitely possible and plausible future will become clearer to you. This creates a power in you that most don't have. It is an evolved power, one in which you can take back control of the issues that are troubling you. Runic magic allows you to commit to living your life with a specific goal in mind and gives a clear set of directions on reaching that goal. The ancient Vikings knew that there were parts of genuinely magical people, and runes allow you to display that magic. They believed in the power of the spoken word and in manifestations way before they became modern concepts.

Runic magic does not look the same for everyone. Because it is such a personal journey, your runes will begin to take on parts of your personality, and your personality will take on parts of your runes. Suppose you are inherently a direct communicative person. In that case, your runes are more likely to give you straightforward answers and encourage you to nurture your intuitive side. Suppose you are an opposing personality to what we've mentioned. In that case, your runes may enhance your intuition and encourage you to be more direct and communicative of what you require. These magical properties that make you uniquely you are gifts given to you by the fates. They are the opportunities bestowed upon you at birth when your true destiny was assigned to you. The fates intended for you to achieve greatness, and when you begin to allow them to speak to you through your runes, that greatness becomes achievable.

Runic was a language that was meant to surpass purely being a form of written or verbal communication. It transcended the physical and connected human beings with the

Conclusion

fates, the gods, their own intuition, and inner magic. While the tales of necromancy and black magic may be off-putting to some, they are a testament to the power of runic magic. Like all fables, some of what was told may be true, and some may have been embellished to warn against using runes and their power for bad rather than good. Whatever the reason behind these tales, the message is clear. Runes and runic magic can change a person's fate. Runes can connect the past, present, and future in a way that paints a picture for the reader and brings every outcome into a clear view. Runic magic's intention was never to harm but offer guidance and protection to those who sought it out. The song to those souls traveling into Valhalla and the light in the dark for the living souls who feel lost. It's about unlocking the magic an ancient tribe instinctively knew was a birthright to all and a guide to the intuition so many choose to ignore. Runic magic is the miracles some people speak of, the manifestations others testify to, and the intuition most of us long to be in tune with.

References

Amy, F. D. (2019, July 14). Runic Magic: The Origin of Runes. Fulldark. https://www.fulldarkpros.com/single-post/2019/07/14/runic-magic-the-origin-of-runes

Chen, M. (2017, March 10). An Introduction to runes. Medium. https://medium.com/@yearlyhoroscope/an-introduction-to-runes-dbddcc2410c0

Cooper, D. J. (2019). Introduction to Runes. Sunnyway.Com. http://www.sunnyway.com/runes/intro.html

Groeneveld, E. (2018, June 19). Runes. Ancient History Encyclopedia; Ancient History Encyclopedia. https://www.ancient.eu/runes/

Gronitz, D. (1999). The Rune Site | Elder Futhark – Rune Meanings. Www.Therunesite.Com. http://www.therunesite.com/elder-futhark-rune-meanings/

Historical Centre, N. (n.d.). Runer og magi. Avaldsnes. https://avaldsnes.info/en/viking/lorem-ipsum/

Magic of Runes - Learn the runic Magic - Talisman & Amulet. (n.d.). Tirage-Rune-Magie.Net. Retrieved November 5, 2020, from http://tirage-rune-magie.net/us/rune/runic-magic.htm

McCoy, D. (2012). The Meanings of the Runes. Norse

References

Mythology for Smart People. https://norse-mythology.org/runes/the-meanings-of-the-runes/

Newton, Dr. S. (n.d.). An Introduction to Runes and Rune Lore – Wuffing Education. Www.Wuffingeducation.Com. Retrieved November 5, 2020, from https://wuffingeducation.co.uk/information/events/2016b/runes/

Rune Stones - Oracles of Divination - Crystalinks. (n.d.). Www.Crystalinks.Com. Retrieved November 5, 2020, from https://www.crystalinks.com/runes.html

Runestones: Words from the Viking Age. (2013, April 4). REAL SCANDINAVIA. http://realscandinavia.com/runestones-words-from-the-viking-age/

The History of Runes. (2015, October 9). Rune Divination. https://runedivination.com/the-history-of-runes/

(The Rune Site | Formerly Ankou's Page of Runes, n.d.)

Tradesman, N. (2020, July 3). how to read norse runes. Norse Tradesman. https://www.norsetradesman.com/blogs/news/how-to-read-runes

Tyson, D. (1988). Runelore and Reading the Runes. Wiccanone.Org.Uk. http://wiccanone.org.uk/rune.html

About the Author

Monique Joiner Siedlak is a writer, witch, and warrior on a mission to awaken people to their greatest potential through the power of storytelling infused with mysticism, modern paganism, and new age spirituality. At the young age of 12, she began rigorously studying the fascinating philosophy of Wicca. By the time she was 20, she was self-initiated into the craft, and hasn't looked back ever since. To this day, she has authored over 40 books pertaining to the magick and mysteries of life.

To find out more about Monique Joiner Siedlak artistically, spiritually, and personally, feel free to visit her **official website**.

www.mojosiedlak.com

facebook.com/mojosiedlak
twitter.com/mojosiedlak
instagram.com/mojosiedlak
pinterest.com/mojosiedlak
bookbub.com/authors/monique-joiner-siedlak

More Books by Monique

African Spirituality Beliefs and Practices
Hoodoo
Seven African Powers: The Orishas
Cooking for the Orishas
Lucumi: The Ways of Santeria
Voodoo of Louisiana
Haitian Vodou
Orishas of Trinidad
Connecting With Your Ancestors
Black Magic
The Orishas

Practical Magick
Wiccan Basics
Candle Magick
Wiccan Spells
Love Spells
Abundance Spells
Herb Magick
Moon Magick

More Books by Monique

Creating Your Own Spells
Gypsy Magic
Protection Magick
Celtic Magick

Personal and Self Development

Creative Visualization
Astral Projection for Beginners
Meditation for Beginners
Reiki for Beginners
Manifesting With the Law of Attraction
Stress Management
Being an Empath Today

Get a Handle on Life

Get a Handle on Anxiety
Get a Handle on Depression
Get a Handle on Procrastination

The Yoga Collective

Yoga for Beginners
Yoga for Stress
Yoga for Back Pain
Yoga for Weight Loss
Yoga for Flexibility
Yoga for Advanced Beginners
Yoga for Fitness
Yoga for Runners
Yoga for Energy
Yoga for Your Sex Life
Yoga to Beat Depression and Anxiety
Yoga for Menstruation
Yoga to Detox Your Body
Yoga to Tone Your Body

More Books by Monique

A Natural Beautiful You
    Creating Your Own Body Butter
    Creating Your Own Body Scrub
    Creating Your Own Body Spray

WANT TO BE FIRST TO KNOW?!

JOIN MY NEWSLETTER

ROSEMAECOOPER.COM/NEWSLETTER

**Thank you for reading my book!
I really appreciate all of your feedback and I love to hear what you have to say.
Please leave your review at your favorite retailer!**

www.ingramcontent.com/pod-product-compliance
Lightning Source LLC
Chambersburg PA
CBHW060845050426
42453CB00008B/835